ADVANCED

Reader's Digest

READING
skill Builder™

PROJECT EDITOR: **WARREN J. HALLIBURTON**

EDITOR: **ELIZABETH GHAFFARI**

CONSULTANTS:

Jorge Garcia, Ed. D.
Supervisor Secondary Reading
Hillsborough County Public
Schools
Tampa, Florida

Susan Pasquini
Reading Specialist/
English Instructor
Escondido High School
San Diego, California

Frank Vernol
Instructional Learning
Secondary Reading
Dallas Independent School
District
Dallas, Texas

Grace Whittaker
Secondary Reading Supervisor
Boston Public Schools
Boston, Massachusetts

READER'S DIGEST EDUCATIONAL DIVISION
The credits and acknowledgments that appear on the inside
back cover are hereby made a part of this copyright page.

Reader's Digest ® Trademark Reg. U.S. Pat. Off. Marca Registrada ISBN 0-88300-275-1

silver edition

□□□ □□□ □ Part 4   Reorder No. B25

CONTENTS

  Stories for which Audio Lessons are available.

Mel Brooks: King of Clowns

Maurice Zolotow

Mel Brooks is a compact man with sad blue eyes and black hair. He has a wide, stretched mouth out of which flows a stream of jokes, wild and lunatic. He exhales gags as casually as air. Until a few years ago, this crazy quipster was known and loved mainly by a small circle of show-business celebrities. He had a reputation as an inventor of bizarre lines and sketches for television comedian Sid Caesar. He also had recorded, with Carl Reiner, some impromptu question-and-answer sessions that became hit comedy records.

Brooks' most famous impersonation is of a 2000-year-old man with a thick Jewish accent:

> Q. *Pardon me, but did you know Napoleon?*
> A. *Yes.*

Q. *How did you meet him?*

A. *Well, I had this summer cottage on Elba. I ran into this little guy on the beach. He was crying. I told him, "So they took France away from you. Don't cry. Go back and recapture it."*

Q. *So you were responsible for his defeat at Waterloo?*

A. *Who, me? Nah, I'm not responsible. You don't listen to every nut on a beach who tells you to go take France back.*

In 1974 Mel Brooks finally found in the movies the audience which had been seeking his kind of insane humor. There had been nothing quite like it since the Marx Brothers and Laurel and Hardy stopped making comedies years ago. His first hits were *Blazing Saddles* (a crazy Western-type comedy) and *Young Frankenstein* (a crazy horror-type comedy). With *Silent Movie* (a crazy silent-movie-type comedy) and *High Anxiety* (a crazy Hitchcock-suspense comedy) added to those first hits, Brooks has become one of the hottest personalities in pictures. He directs and helps write all his films. Often he is also one of the stars.

In a time when movies are often about disaster, sex, blood and misery, Mel Brooks has dared to return to the early slapstick of films. He has gone back to the world of Mack Sennett and pie throwing and clowning.

So come with me into the world of Mel Brooks. Get your mind off killer sharks, burning skyscrapers, wars in outer space and the rotten people of the world.

Mel Brooks' office is a huge corner suite in the executive building on the Twentieth Century-Fox lot in West Los Angeles. To visitors, Mel gives out chocolate-coated raisins. He munches them himself, and he gave some to me. Why raisins? "Well, what did you expect, tea and cucumber sandwiches? Sherry and biscuits? Here we give raisins."

One of his interviewers spurned the raisins. Mel said he should at least take a few boxes home for his children. "No," the man said. "Chocolate is bad for teeth."

"Are teeth so good for chocolate?" snarled Mel.

Cleavon Little in *Blazing Saddles*

I was coughing. A chewed raisin stuck in my throat. "Eat them, eat them, they're good for you," he chortled. "They are nutritious. Whatever damage the chocolate is doing, the raisins are correcting. There's iron in them."

"Iron?"

"Yes. The only problem is that you can't stay in the water too long if you're a raisin eater because you rust."

"How do you overcome the rust problem?"

"I DRINK OIL!" he cried at once.

This impromptu exchange brings out two points about Mel's comedy. One, it arises out of everyday situations. Two, it is a comedy of exaggeration, wandering between fantasy and reality.

Both forms of comedy appear in a scene from *Blazing Saddles*, one of Mel's most successful movies, when a chain-gang boss tells the prisoners to sing a typical work song. They burst into song with Cole Porter's "I Get a Kick Out of You," accompanied by Count Basie's 24-piece orchestra sitting on a flatcar out in the Western badlands of the 1880s.

Mel Brooks, incidentally, used to be a professional jazz drummer and loves the Ellington, Armstrong and Basie kind of jazz. He writes his own movie theme songs and admires the singing of Sinatra, Crosby and Fred Astaire. When he drives around town, Mel likes to play tapes of Astaire singing. His car, by the way, is a Honda. He used to drive a Buick. He says that where he grew up in Brooklyn, Buick was everybody's status car.

"So," I inquired, "has the Honda become a status car?"

"No," he shot back. "The Honda is for tall people who want to look short."

"But, Mel, you *are* short."

"You see, it works, it works."

Mel Brooks is never at a loss for a comeback. After paying Mel a minimal $500 for a guest appearance on a television show, David Frost said to him: "I guess you're giving the fee to your favorite charity."

"Yes," Mel rasped. "I'm donating it to my left pocket." (In truth, he is charitable.)

Movie critics do not, Mel believes, sympathize with or understand what he is doing. Asked once, "What do you think of the critics?" he answered, "They're very noisy at night. You can't sleep in the country because of them."

"Isn't that *crickets* you're talking about? I meant *critics.*"

"Oh, *critics!* What good are they? They can't make music with their hind legs."

Mel Brooks was born Melvin Kaminsky, youngest of four brothers, in a poverty-stricken Jewish quarter of Brooklyn, New York, in 1926.

Mel's comedy has been seen by some as a reaction to growing up in a Jewish "ghetto" environment. But his humor is definitely not in the tradition of "Jewish humor." His comedy has more of the brashness of frontier American humor, like the early sketches of Bret Harte and Mark Twain.

How did raw American frontier humor come to infect this kid from Brooklyn? Through the silent movies. Through the crude silent-movie comedies of Mack Sennett, Fatty Arbuckle and other clowns.

When Mel was a boy during the 1930s, a dozen or so cafes and restaurants on and off the famous boardwalk at Coney Island in New York City showed silent movies to attract customers. There was no admission. You sat down in a semi-darkened room of round tables and wooden chairs, ordered a hot dog and a root beer, and could watch a flickering classic by Chaplin or see the Keystone Kops. As long as you had something on the table, they didn't throw you out. I know. I was taken to such places by my mother, as Mel was by his.

"I fell in love with movies right there," he told me. "Outside, life was dirty and hard. My mother had to work ten hours a day to support the family. Kids beat me up because I was a shrimp. I knew I was ugly and no good. But in here, in the dark, I could eat a hot dog and drink root beer and it was beautiful. This was much better than real life. Who needs real life?

"Later, when I was old enough to go to pictures alone, I had a big diet of Western movies and talking pictures in a dump neighborhood theater. My mother was always sending an older brother to drag me out. Sometimes I went there when it opened, 11:30 in the morning, and stayed until nightfall. I could be starved to death, have a splitting headache, but I couldn't take my eyes off the screen. This was my school—the movies."

He also attended Eastern District High School, graduating in 1944. Then he spent 2½ years in the Army. A good part of that time he was in Europe with a combat-engineer outfit assigned to move ahead of the armies and repair broken bridges and power stations. Of that experience, Mel says, "It was very unhealthy work."

After his discharge, Brooks became a professional drummer. He also started saying clever things and got laughs. Then in the Catskill Mountains (a resort area in New York State) one summer, he fell in with another musician, a tenor saxophonist named Sid Caesar. They became friends. Or, rather, Sid Caesar became a star of television comedy, with Your Show of Shows (on from 1950 to 1954), and Mel Brooks was his court jester.

Brooks, at first, was barely tolerated by the rest of the show's staff. He was always late. He was always impudent and impertinent, a restless, nervous person. He couldn't sit at a typewriter. But he could, running about, spout out jokes that were perfect for Caesar. And if you didn't like this Brooks idea or gag, he had ten others.

When Your Show of Shows ended, Mel went through a long period of defeats and struggle. He wrote a Broadway show that flopped. He couldn't get a comedy-writing job because he was known to be cantankerous. His first marriage was breaking up. (Today he is married to actress Anne Bancroft, and they have one of the most enchanting relationships I've ever known.) He was suffering from severe emotional problems, for which he was treated for six years.

His symptoms were relieved, and he began to get some emotional maturity. But he was still hard-pressed financially. In 1965 Brooks and writer-actor Buck Henry started the Get Smart television series. Then Mel decided he wanted to direct and write movies, and

Sid Caesar and Imogene Coca in scene from "Your Show of Shows"

write novels. He started writing a novel, *Springtime for Hitler*. It later became his first film, *The Producers* (1967).

The Producers died at the box office, and it took three years to get another backer for a movie: *The Twelve Chairs*. It, too, laid a colossal egg, and it took four years to get out another film. This one, *Blazing Saddles*, made his fortune.

Now, after the successes of his recent films, Mel Brooks is able to write his own ticket in Hollywood. He oversees every part of his films, even the sound track.

I first met this man when we were both young. He was wild and undisciplined and, yes, also lovable and outrageously funny. How this Mel Brooks I remember became the disciplined and orderly person he is today, I don't know.

But that's what happened. An even greater miracle is that along the way he has not lost his naturalness, his creative madness, his love of life and people. He gets his hard work done, amid phone interruptions, in an office that is usually full of friends. How does he do it? Maybe it's the raisins.

As I was leaving Brooks' office, I admired a picture of him in a blazer and yachting cap. "Handsome man, isn't he?" said Brooks thoughtfully. "If only I looked like him, I could be a movie star!"

Number of Words: 1994 ÷ _____ Minutes Reading Time = Rate _____

I. AUTHOR'S PURPOSE

The selection brings Mel Brooks' personality to life for the reader. Check √ three statements below that show how the author does this.

_____ **1.** The author tells us in detail how Mel Brooks writes movie scripts.

_____ **2.** The author uses actual dialogue to show that Mel is never at a loss for a funny remark.

_____ **3.** The author gives us his own opinions about how Mel should lead his life.

_____ **4.** The author describes Mel's childhood to show how the boy grew up to be a comedian.

_____ **5.** The author helps us to understand Mel by telling about many different aspects of his life.

_____ **6.** The author describes Mel's schooling to show how it prepared Mel to be a successful maker of funny movies.

_____ **7.** The author quotes the many anecdotes of Mel's relatives reflecting on his behavior.

10 points for each correct answer   SCORE: _____

II. CLASSIFYING

At one time or another during his life, Mel Brooks has been many things. Check √ five that are mentioned in the selection.

_____ **1.** a jazz drummer
_____ **2.** a pop singer
_____ **3.** a comedy writer
_____ **4.** a filmmaker
_____ **5.** a cook

_____ **6.** a teacher
_____ **7.** an avid moviegoer
_____ **8.** a concert pianist
_____ **9.** a recording artist
_____ **10.** a disc jockey

4 points for each correct answer   SCORE: _____

III. INFERENCES

Check √ four statements below that can be inferred from the story.

_____ **1.** Mel can probably think of something funny to say about almost anything.

_____ **2.** Mel's humor is often based on the absurd.

_____ **3.** Mel's humor is usually cruel to other people.

_____ **4.** Mel's humor uses visual as well as verbal techniques.

_____ **5.** Mel was funny only when he had problems.

_____ **6.** He is not above misusing words or making puns.

5 points for each correct answer   SCORE: _____

IV. LANGUAGE USAGE

Match the author's expressions describing how Mel talks (column A) with their meanings (column B).

	A		B
_____ **1.**	chortled	**a.**	laughed quietly
_____ **2.**	rasped	**b.**	told jokes constantly
_____ **3.**	exhales gags	**c.**	growled
		d.	breathes humor
_____ **4.**	snarled	**e.**	said in a grating voice
_____ **5.**	spouted out jokes		

6 points for each correct answer   SCORE: _____

PERFECT TOTAL SCORE: 100   TOTAL SCORE: _____

V. QUESTION FOR THOUGHT

How do you think you would feel being around someone with Mel Brooks' personality?

"A Very Lucky Individual"
Seamus McGrady

Early one Sunday morning last June, the Charles Warnock family left their home in Bremerton, Washington, for an outing at nearby Olympic National Park. The two Warnock boys—Chuck, 18, and Donny, 16—planned to swim down Staircase Rapids. This fast chute of water would be ideal, they hoped, for their favorite sport, which combines the thrills of body surfing and river rafting.

The Warnocks left their car near the park ranger station, then hiked the mile up to the head of the rapids, arriving shortly after noon. It was a hot, sunny day, and Chuck, wearing his wet-suit jacket and gloves, quickly slipped into a quiet pool. When the shock of the icy water wore off, he relaxed and, feet first, let the current carry him downstream. Nearing the white water, he whooped with expectation.

Standing on a large boulder overlooking the pool, Donny watched his brother approach a small waterfall. Suddenly, noticing some large rocks at the bottom of the falls, he yelled, "Stop! It's too dangerous!"

Chuck tried to brace his wiry 5-foot-8-inch (173-centimeter), 120-pound (54-kilogram) frame against the flow of water, but his shoes skidded on the slick pebbles. He made an attempt to grab onto a rock, but his mitten-like gloves slipped on the wet moss and he shot head over heels down the cascading white water.

Donny scrambled off his perch and checked below the falls. "Dad!" he shouted, "Chuck went under and hasn't come up yet."

When he heard Donny call, Charles Warnock left his wife, Carol, and rushed to the riverbank. He remembers thinking: *He probably just stayed under longer than expected. He'll turn up farther down the river.* Then, about 15 yards (14 meters) upstream, he saw Chuck's glove pop to the surface. *He must be caught under a rock. Why else would he lose his glove?* "Donny," he called, "run to the ranger station and get help."

12

Leaping from rock to rock, the distraught father tried to race straight up the river to the waterfall about 100 feet (30 meters) away. *How long could Chuck last? A minute? Two?* The water became deeper and swifter. Making his way to a huge boulder in the middle of the river, he tried to probe beneath the boiling rapids with a long stick. He found nothing. Minutes sped by. A hiker on the trail gave Carol Warnock a 25-foot (7.6-meter) rope, which she threw out to her husband. Warnock lassoed a log caught between two rocks at the head of the waterfall and wrapped the other end around his hand.

Slowly, he inched his way down the left side of the boulder. *If he's there—and conscious—he might try to grab my legs, and I could pull him out.* He came to the end of the rope, his legs feeling nothing but water and stone. He pulled himself back up.

Next he went down the right side of the boulder. When he came to the end of the rope this time, the force of the river made him lose his footing, but he held on with both hands. He thought: *He has to be right down there, and I can't even reach him. I could let go, but it wouldn't help—there would be two dead instead of one.* It took all his strength for Warnock to work his way to the top again.

Carol Warnock called out to her husband: "Do you see him?"

"No. But stay away! The river's too fast here."

Carol felt her stomach tighten. *There must be something he doesn't want me to see,* she thought. *Something terrible.*

At 12:55 the park rangers arrived, and, despite the fact that Chuck had been missing since 12:15, they began a "hasty search," which meant covering the area as rapidly as possible in hopes of finding a person instead of a body.

Ranger Andy Cohen tied two climbing ropes around his waist and quickly entered the water where Warnock had been looking. He realized that chances of finding Chuck alive were "slim to none," but hurried from pool to pool anyway, crossing and recrossing the churning river. Cohen used his hands and feet and short sticks to search around and beneath rocks and overhanging ledges. Behind the largest boulders, the suction was so great he had to be hauled out bodily by the rangers at the ends of his ropes. After 45 minutes, Cohen struggled ashore and nearly collapsed. The rangers called off the hasty search.

After his tumble down the cascade, Chuck had surfaced inside a cave-like air pocket beneath a huge boulder at the foot of the falls. He felt all right—at least nothing was broken—and he had air to breathe. When his eyes adjusted to the darkness, he could see that his little chamber was about three feet (91 centimeters) wide and six feet (183 centimeters) long. He saw no escape route other than leaving the way he had come in, which meant going almost straight up a narrow passage of churning water. To get a better grip, he took off his gloves and stuck them inside his jacket. One of them fell out. Standing tiptoe on a small rock, he grabbed a ledge near the opening and tried to pull himself up. The frothing waterfall pushed him down and back into the hollow. He hit his head on the way in.

He paused to catch his

breath before making a second attempt. Getting out, he realized, would be more difficult than he had imagined. *If only I can get up high enough to yell, somebody might hear and come take me out.* He pulled himself up as high as he could, but he discovered he could not breathe, much less shout. Worn out, he let the swirling water carry him to the rear of the cave. There was no light back there, and no sign of an exit anywhere.

He rested and tried to think clearly. He knew he had strength left for only one more try. Perhaps if he reduced the drag of his body, he could

make it. He took off his wet-suit jacket and set it on a log. Shivering, he swam quickly to the entrance, grabbed the ledge and heaved. Once again he was forced back into his cell.

Chuck managed to get back into his jacket, but it brought no warmth. Its buoyancy, however, helped him stay afloat. He draped his arms over a log and locked his fingers together. The light seemed to grow dimmer, the air heavier. He fell asleep.

After resting, Ranger Cohen had reentered the river for the "thorough search" phase of the operation. Wearing a wet suit and face mask, he worked carefully and slowly, reaching as far as he could into each crevice and under every rock. Despite the mask, the visibility was poor. The afternoon sun had melted the snow in the mountains, and the river was higher and more turbulent than it had been. Cohen wondered how the parents would react when they saw their son's body.

Soon the sun dipped beneath the park's towering fir and cedar trees, and the air grew chilly. Head Ranger George Bowen had stationed observers along the banks of the river, hoping that the afternoon's rising water level would dislodge the body from its hiding place. Now, back at the ranger station, he began planning for the next day's search. At daybreak, there would be fresh men in complete scuba gear ready to take advantage of the lowest water. *If necessary, we'll turn over every rock in the river. But we will find him.* He told the Warnocks his men would soon have to give up the search for the day.

"No matter how long it takes," Warnock told his wife, "I can't leave here until he's found."

"Neither can I," she said.

When Chuck opened his eyes, the cave was pitch black. The water swirling at the entrance now came up to his chin. The air seemed dense, and it was hard to breathe. He was cold and, despite his nap, felt exhausted.

Knowing it would be useless to try to pull himself up the waterfall again, he began exploring every inch of the cave. Finally, near the back, he felt an indentation he had not noticed before. Was this a possible means of escape from his stone prison? He stuck his leg in as far as he could and met no resistance. *It could be a way out, or I could get stuck in there. But I can't hold out much longer here.*

He took a deep breath and squeezed his body down into the opening. Immediately, the current forced him through and out into the river. He shot to the surface, to the light and the sweet, fresh air. Alive and free, Chuck could not remember ever being so happy. He swam to a rock and clung to it.

Andy Cohen, resting on the bank after fighting the river for almost three hours, wondered if he should go in for one more try. He told Cal Early, a ranger who had been pulling him out of the water all afternoon, "It would be different if we were looking for somebody alive. But for a body. . . ."

Early interrupted, pointing out at the river, "Who's that?"

Cohen saw someone in the middle of the river crouching on a boulder. *Oh, no. That's all we need—some overeager bystander trying to help.* "What are you doing out there?" he demanded. Then he looked again, remembering a photo Charles Warnock had shown him. "It's him! It's him!" he yelled.

Cohen and Early hit the water at the same time. Cohen grabbed Chuck and tied a rope around his waist. Early clambered up the boulder and slowly hauled Chuck to the top. Cohen, an emergency medical technician, joined them and examined Chuck. "How do you feel?" he asked.

"Hungry," Chuck said. Then

he fainted.

In the ranger station, a quiet voice came over the radio: "We found him." There was a pause, then, triumphantly, "And he's alive!"

Carol Warnock felt tears roll down her cheeks. "Thank God," she murmured. "Oh, thank you, God." She put her arms around her husband and they both wept. Their tears were of gratitude.

Cohen was afraid they might yet lose Chuck. The youth's pupils were fixed and dilated. His skin was bluish, his pulse weak and his breathing shallow. Cohen and Early carried Chuck to the closer riverbank, lay down beside him and hugged him to keep him warm. Whenever Chuck was conscious, Cohen tried to feed him hot coffee and chocolate, but his patient had difficulty keeping the food down. Finally emergency equipment—warm clothing, blankets, a stretcher and oxygen—arrived from the ranger station. Only then, when the youth was breathing the pure oxygen, did Cohen know the worst was over.

It was difficult carrying Chuck by stretcher through trailless woods to the ranger station. But Cohen recalls it as

the "most joyous hike" he had ever been on. When the Warnocks finally met their son and the rangers about a quarter-mile (0.4 kilometer) from the station, there was not a dry eye among them. But they were smiling and joking, too. Carrying the stretcher and still wearing his wet suit, Cohen inquired, "Who's going to sign for this package?"

At 6:05 Chuck and his mother were flown to a medical center by a rescue helicopter. Chuck spent the night there and was released the next afternoon.

Although Chuck has gained a healthy respect for the dangers of swimming down rapids, he won't give up the sport. "The Staircase Rapids is too rocky and too fast," he says. "I won't do that one again. But you don't give up driving a car because you've had one accident, do you?"

Perhaps the last word belongs to Head Ranger Bowen, who concluded his report with this simple observation: "A very lucky individual."

Number of Words: 2007 ÷ _____ Minutes Reading Time = Rate _____

I. SEQUENCE

The statements below describe events that happened in the story. Number them in the order they occurred.

_____ **a.** The current forced Chuck out of the cave.

_____ **b.** Chuck shot over the waterfall and disappeared.

_____ **c.** The park rangers were ready to give up the search for the day.

_____ **d.** A happy but exhausted Chuck was finally rescued by the rangers.

_____ **e.** Donny shouted a warning to his brother.

_____ **f.** Chuck was reunited with his family.

_____ **g.** Donny reported the accident to his father.

5 points for each correct answer   SCORE: _____

II. PROBLEM SOLVING

The following are actions that might be taken in a rescue effort similar to the one in the story. Check √ two actions that would be helpful and leave blank each that would make matters worse.

_____ **1.** Jump into the water to look for the missing person.

_____ **2.** Tie one end of a rope around a tree and the other end around the waist before entering the water.

_____ **3.** Wave a life-preserver over the water, and shout.

_____ **4.** Get help from rangers or policemen.

_____ **5.** Get as many people as possible into the water.

_____ **6.** Build a small raft suitable for riding rapids.

5 points for each correct answer   SCORE: _____

III. CAUSE/EFFECT

Some of the actions that Chuck took caused the events in the selection to happen. Match each cause (column A) to its effect (column B). Write the letter in the space provided.

	A		B
_____ **1.**	He had used up most of the air in the cave.	**a.**	He fell over the waterfall.
_____ **2.**	He found an opening to squeeze through.	**b.**	He took off his wet suit.
_____ **3.**	He wanted to reduce the drag of the water on his body.	**c.**	He found it hard to breathe.
_____ **4.**	He slid on the slippery rocks.	**d.**	He escaped.

10 points for each correct answer   SCORE: _____

IV. CHARACTERIZATION

Circle the letter for the one word that best describes the behavior of each of the following persons in the story.

1. Chuck   **a.** determined **b.** foolhardy **c.** agitated
2. Charles Warnock **a.** indifferent **b.** angry   **c.** distressed
3. Andy Cohen   **a.** courageous **b.** humorous   **c.** undecided

5 points for each correct answer   SCORE: _____

PERFECT TOTAL SCORE: 100   TOTAL SCORE: _____

V. QUESTIONS FOR THOUGHT

If you had been stuck in the cave instead of Chuck, would you have done anything differently? What? Explain why.

MY LIFE IN PRO BALL

Bill Bradley

What is it like to be a professional athlete? Is it a life of glamour and $30,000 TV endorsements? Or a life of constant travel and long, aching nights in look-alike hotel rooms?

Bill Bradley—a graduate of Princeton University, All American basketball player, Rhodes Scholar, former forward for the New York Knickerbockers professional basketball team, and United States Senator—answers these questions with unusual frankness and insight in his book *Life on the Run*.

The phone rings. I roll over in bed and grab the receiver. The motel operator says, "Wake-up call. It's 9 a.m. Your bus leaves at ten." We are in Cleveland, where last night we—the New York Knicks—lost to the Cleveland Cavaliers. Outside, a cold drizzle soaks the city. I draw a hot bath and sit in it for five minutes to loosen my body's stiffness. My socks, shoes and Knick uniform hang drying over the chairs, the room heater, the floor lamp. My mouth is dry and burning. My legs ache. I've slept poorly.

Next day, Tuesday, we play at home. Before the game at Madison Square Garden, an avid fan tells me the Knicks give him something to look forward to after a day at work in the post office. I am his favorite player. He is similar to other fans who have identified with the team and me. They suffer with us when we lose, and they are ecstatic when we win. They are the bedrock of our experience as professional players.

That night we win by 20 points. After the game I take a long shower. Then I stuff my wet socks, my shoes and my underwear into the traveling bag with my road uniform for the bus ride to the airport.

We land in Atlanta at 1 a.m. It is 21° Fahrenheit (-6° Celsius) outside, and the frost makes the runway sparkle as if it were sprinkled with bits of glass. We wait 40 minutes for our bags, which delays our arrival at the hotel until 3 a.m.

There is an overpowering loneliness on the road. A local acquaintance may show up during the day. There is chit-chat with him of times past and of his job and my activities outside of basketball. After that exchange, there is nothing more to say, little common interest. Sometimes I take in an art exhibit or visit an unusual section of town. Or I sit in a hotel room reading books, listening to the radio.

Someday, I say to myself, I won't be spending 100 days a year on the road. Someday I'll wake up in the same place every morning. I miss that sense of sharing that comes from people living together in one place, over time. I miss permanence.

From Atlanta we fly to Chicago. I go to a luncheon where I am the principal speaker. About 200 men attend. Part of being a professional basketball player is speaking at shopping-center openings, charity fund-raisers, sports banquets and annual company dinners. The audience laughs at my jokes. Even unfunny stories told by athletes make audiences roll in the aisles.

We lose to the Chicago Bulls by 16 points. Our plane touches down in New York at 3:45 a.m. The doorman of my apartment building tells me he is sorry about the loss in Chicago, but he made $100 betting against us. I get into bed around 5:30 a.m. Just one more game this week, then we have two days off. We will have played five games in seven days in four different cities.

Saturday does not begin for me until 1 p.m. Whenever we return from a road trip late, the next day is always a jumble. At 3 p.m. I have my usual pregame steak-and-salad meal. (I will not eat again until midnight supper after the game.) I sleep for an hour. The alarm goes off at six. I arrive at Madison Square Garden just one hour before the game.

The locker room has become a kind of home for me. I often enter tense and uneasy, bothered by some event of the day. Slowly my worries fade as I see their unimportance to my teammates. I relax, my concerns lost among the everyday exchanges of an athlete's life. Athletes may be crude and immature, but they are genuine when it comes to loyalty, responsibility and honesty. The members of my team have seen me, and I them, in more moods and tough spots than I care to remember. Our lives intertwine far beyond the court. It is a good life with pleasant people. If victory and unity fuse on one team, life becomes a joy. It is a life that truly makes sense only while you're living it.

I tape my ankles and put on my uniform. Then I turn to the mail that has just been delivered. I usually get about 40 letters a week, almost none of them from people I know. There are requests for a few autographs.

The last letter I open is from Kentucky. It is from the father of a boy whom I had met when he was a sophomore at the University of Kentucky. He came all the way from Kentucky to ask me to show him how to shoot a basketball. He just appeared at my apartment one day. We went up to Riverside Park, talked and shot baskets for about an hour. He thanked me for the help and boarded a

bus back home. I saw him later that year in Cincinnati. He had been cut from the Kentucky team. He was down, and convinced that his sprained ankle had something to do with it.

I wrote him a letter two years later, after his sister had written that he had cancer. The boy's father thanks me for the letter but says that his son has died. I put the letter down. Coach "Red" Holzman begins his pre-game conversation. I can't concentrate. I should have written sooner. I feel numbed with anger and sorrow.

From the middle of September until May, there is usually no longer than one day at a time without basketball. There are no long weekends or national holidays for players. It is impossible to take a trip to the mountains or fly to Florida even for two days. We are a part of show business, providing public entertainment. We work on Christmas night and New Year's Eve.

We arrive in Los Angeles for the first stop of a five-game western trip. My normal routine the day before a game in another town is to find a facility where I can get a steam bath, whirlpool and massage. Games and practices bring injuries, and travel brings fatigue.

A professional basketball player must be able to run six miles in a game, 100 times a year—jumping and pivoting under continuous physical contact. The body is constantly battered and ground away. During this year alone I have had a jammed finger, an injured arch, a smashed nose cartilage, five split lips, an elbow in the throat that eliminated my voice for a week, a bruised right hip, a sprained ankle, a left hip joint out of socket and a bruised left wrist.

Every workout brings the fear of re-injury, and every night brings the hope for tomorrow's improvement. I wake up in the middle of the night and flex my knee to see if there is pain, or knead my thigh to see if the charley horse has begun to heal.

I often ask myself why I continue to play. In 1967, when I first signed, I was convinced that I would play no more than four years, the length of my initial contract. I'm still playing. One reason is the money. The average salary in the National Basketball Association (NBA) is close to $100,000. Many players make more than $150,000. There is no question that it gives me a sense of security and a greater feeling of freedom, mobility and accomplishment. But money is not the only reason I play. The answer lies much deeper in the workings of the game and in me.

I recall, for about the 50th time this season, how it was in 1970, the first time we won the NBA championship. I stood at mid-court in Madison Square Garden, New York, two fists raised, chills coursing up and down my spine. Since I was nine years old, I had played basketball to become the best. Individual honors were nice but not enough. An Olympic gold medal gave satisfaction, but it was not top-flight basketball. The NBA was clearly the highest caliber in the world, and there I was, a part of the best team.

I remembered all those statements of team unity expressed since high school; all the hours of loneliness, dribbling and shooting a basketball in a gym somewhere in the world. I recalled all the near misses in the smaller championships—high school and college, all the missed opportunities in other fields. I looked back on all the denied personal enjoyment, all the conflicts suppressed and angers swallowed. Everything seemed worth it for the feeling at center court on May 8, 1970.

In those few moments after victory, in the locker room with the team, there was a total oneness with the world. Owners and politicians celebrate in the locker room of a champion. But only the players, the coach and perhaps the trainer can feel the special satisfaction of the achievement. They start nine months earlier, in training camp. They play the games, endure the travel. They receive the public criticism and overcome their own personal ambitions. The high of the championship is unequaled. The possibility that it could happen again is enough lure to continue. The money is important, but the chance to relive that moment outweighs dollars.

Prepared to live without the game

But how fast it is gone!

On a flight to Phoenix, I open a magazine to a story about Mickey Mantle at his home in Dallas, Texas, after several years out of baseball.

"I loved it," the author quotes Mantle as saying, his voice throbbing with intensity. "Nobody could have loved playing ball as much as me, when I wasn't hurt. I must have 50 scrapbooks. Sometimes after breakfast, I sit by myself and take a scrapbook and just turn the pages. The hair comes up on the back of my neck. I get goose bumps. And I remember how it was and how I used to think that it would always be that way."

The words seem to jump off the page at me. There is terror behind the dream of being a professional ballplayer. It comes as a slow realization of finality and of the frightening unknowns which the end brings. When the playing is over, one can sense that one's youth has been spent playing a game, and now both the game and youth are gone.

By age 35 any possibility for developing skills outside of basketball is slim. What is left is the other side of the bargain: to live all one's days never able to recapture the feeling of those few years of intensified youth. The athlete approaches the end of his playing days the way old people approach death. He puts his finances in order. He reminisces easily. He offers advice to the young. But the athlete differs from an old person in that he must continue living. Behind all the years of practice and all the crowds and hours of glory waits that unavoidable terror of living without the game.

Number of Words: 1925 ÷ _____ Minutes Reading Time = Rate _____

I. STORY ELEMENTS

Check ✓ *four terms below that can be used to describe the selection.*

_____ **1.** thriller   _____ **6.** dialogue
_____ **2.** first person account   _____ **7.** autobiography
_____ **3.** narrative   _____ **8.** legend
_____ **4.** newspaper article   _____ **9.** memoir
_____ **5.** biography   _____ **10.** speech

10 points for each correct answer   SCORE: _____

II. SUPPORTING DETAILS

The selection gives details from the life of a professional basketball player. Circle the letter (a, b or c) of the phrase that best completes each statement below.

1. Bill Bradley plays for the _____ .
  a. Chicago Bulls
  b. Boston Celtics
  c. New York Knicks

2. Most of the time, Bill Bradley's team travels _____ .
  a. by bus
  b. in private cars
  c. late at night

3. During the Christmas holidays, the team may _____ .
  a. play several games
  b. take a trip to Florida
  c. not play

4. In 1970 Bill Bradley _____ .
  a. signed his first contract
  b. was part of the championship team
  c. ended his career

5. When they retire, athletes _____ .
   a. miss their playing days
   b. are sure to find new careers easily
   c. all become managers

6 points for each correct answer   SCORE: _____

III. SUMMARY

Check ✓ six of the following statements that would be included in a short summary of the story.

_____ **1.** Bill Bradley loves to play professional basketball.

_____ **2.** He is the best player around.

_____ **3.** He does not like the life of constant travel.

_____ **4.** His life does not allow him a feeling of permanence.

_____ **5.** He plays basketball only to please the fans.

_____ **6.** He receives many minor injuries each season.

_____ **7.** The high point of his basketball career was winning the NBA championship.

_____ **8.** He is afraid of the day when he will have to retire.

5 points for each correct answer   SCORE: _____

PERFECT TOTAL SCORE: 100   TOTAL SCORE: _____

IV. QUESTIONS FOR THOUGHT

Have you thought about a career in professional sports? Why do you think you would or would not like this type of life?

Jamake Highwater

Marcia Highwater's Native Land

It's 6:19 in the morning when the old lady steps off the airplane. She takes her first dispassionate glance at the New York City skyline as I watch her from behind my glass wall. I am more mystified by her now than when I was a boy—when she used to tell me stories about her mother and father.

She would say to me quietly, "Your grandparents . . . they died . . . of starvation." The corner of her mouth would wince, and leftover grief would fill her dark aristocratic eyes.

Now I am standing behind the huge airport window. I am among the relatives of the other passengers getting off the airplane. Beside these urban travelers, my mother looks a bit like a colorful, overstuffed pillow in her long skirt and Anglo raincoat. And I wonder why Indians in Anglo clothes always remind me of monkeys dressed to perform in dumb shows they have not had a part in creating.

I watch my mother, Marcia Highwater, as she comes down the ramp. When she sees me waiting for her, she allows herself a burst of emotion—a smile. It lasts a moment and then leaps behind a wall of embarrassment. We have communicated through this wall during my entire life.

When I was a child and white kids gave me a rough time because my hair was long, my mother wanted to comfort me. She would murmur in my ear as she laid me down to sleep, "Your grandfather was a fine-looking man. He was not yet 30 when he died. It was a bad winter that year, and by spring my mother too was gone. And then Tantika, my little sister, died of pneumonia. It was a bad winter, my son." She chanted this story like a sad, sad lullaby.

And now Marcia Highwater and I walk through the concrete canyons of Manhattan. At 49th Street and Avenue of the Americas, she stops suddenly and looks up at the sky, as if she were lost, as if she were seeking a familiar landmark.

"Man-hat-tan. It is the name of a people, not a city. It is the name of an Indian people."

"Come, let me get you something to eat," I whisper to her, as people begin to stop and stare at us. She continues to peer into the sky and into the faces of these strangers as I take her hand and urge her to follow me into a cafe.

My mother's luggage is nothing but a single large pull-string bag, which she insists on carrying for herself. I remember she used to say that if she ever brushed the dust from her hands then she wouldn't own anything at all. But actually she was pretty rich for a while—when I was still a boy. After my father died, Mama married a white man, who adopted me and took me into his big house. But he lost most of what they had, and then he died one hot Sunday afternoon.

I remember I once brought some kids home from school. Mama was in the kitchen, cooking dinner. When the kids saw her there, they began to laugh. I couldn't understand why they were laughing. For

many months afterward they would run around me and beat their palms against their mouth, making those terrible "Indian" noises which white people think are so funny. Mama very often cooked solid foods directly on the burners of the stove, without a pot. I thought that everybody's mother prepared dinner in the same way. But I learned that that was a difference between us and the Anglos, and they detest differences. They pity us if we don't possess what they possess. And they dislike us if we do not want the things that would make us the same as them. When you are a child, it is not easy to understand the contempt born of differences.

After dinner I say, "Mama would you like to go to a movie with me?"

"You flew me across the sky to New York City to see a silly movie?"

"No, Mama, this movie is about Indians. It's called *Journey to Rosebud*."

33

"Cowboys and Indians. Huh! John Wayne! No, no movie. We will walk and see these Manhattan people."

And so we slowly make our way toward 59th Street. We are gawked at by little boys with the bewildered faces of children seeing Santa Claus. We are ignored by adult New Yorkers who assume that anybody different is putting on some kind of improper display.

And I remember the faces in the Western films I watched when I was a child, long ago. In a cinder-block living room, I sat with a group of other Indians in the darkness in front of an old blurry television set, watching the "Late, Late Show." John Wayne was leading a cavalry charge against the "savages"—godless, cruel animals sneaking through the tall grass with knives between their teeth. But really they were white men in Hollywood makeup, making fierce faces under phony warbonnets. And there was always the Anglo woman who screamed: "Kill me! Please kill me! You know what they do to women and children!"

I am six years old and I'm convinced that Indians are horrible people. At night I have

nightmares about them. And in the morning when I brush my teeth, I see in the mirror the face that frightened me in my dream. Sometimes I cry.

"What do you think about?" Marcia Highwater asks me, a trace of gentleness appearing briefly in her proud features. "Think about where you are going, not where you have been," she advises.

After a moment I nod and fake a smile. "Yes," I mutter—as if the future can be separated from the past.

"Do not lick wounds which have healed," Mama drones without looking at me. She has always been able to under-

stand what people are thinking. I could never lie to her when I was a child. She reads faces as astronomers read the sky—nothing is too distant for her to see.

She mutters to herself for a moment, looking around, and then she asks: "What have they done with the trees?"

"Well—Mama—let's see—well, they are just up the street. You see—they put them all in Central Park."

"Huh!" she snorts, then remarks "So they put the trees on reservations too!"

"My son," Marcia Highwater says calmly as we join the familiar company of the trees and grass in Central Park, "the white man does not understand the Indian. He knows the Arab in Egypt and the Jew in Israel better than he knows us who live in his midst."

"Do you want him to know about us?" I ask.

"He is here. He will always be here. So it is better that he sees our footprints upon this old land rather than think that America began in 1492. You have your father's way with words, my son, so you must tell them. . . ."

Yes, I must tell them. About the end of the romantic Indian of the poets. About the Indian's simplicity and kinship with nature, which by civilized standards has changed to squalor. And I must ask: Is the hogan, the lodge, the teepee or the shack a proper home in the second half of the 20th century? Or must we all follow like sheep after the Bureau of Indian Affairs, leaving our native homes? Must we move to their cinder-block housing projects, which confine and confuse us more than all the limits and reservations that the white man has used to destroy us?

And I must also ask myself if perhaps, after all, Indians are not a people programmed to die out.

No, I do not believe it! There is a chance that our race of less than a million may have a meaningful impact on the new world. As we face the results of polluting our air and our streams, as we see the terrible effects of unlimited industrial growth, it may dawn upon us that this is the twilight of mankind. It is possible then that the simplicity and respect for nature that touches every part of Indian life may point to a path that leads away from this disastrous course called "progress."

Now the old lady is leaving— my mother looking out into the sky above Manhattan. Perhaps she sees something there that we cannot see. She has always had a mastery of vision. When we were children and we would fight, Mama would sit down with us on the ground, among the walnut trees, her blue and red and orange skirts fanning out like the wings of some immense butterfly. And she would embrace us all and stare off into the sky as she would rock us to and fro, ever so gently. And then she would chant:

O, come little brothers. O, come little sisters.
And let us dance to the drum. For then do we move to the same rhythm.

I will tell them, Marcia Highwater. I will try to tell them about the land and the rivers and the ancient ways of your father and of your father's father. I will lay a wreath on your starved daddy's grave. And the song I will sing is the song that has come down through the generations of us—carried in the very pulse of our cruelly diminished people. It comes from the days when the rivers were clear and the prairie was filled with the buffalo, when the giant redwoods were mere saplings.

That story lives in the Indian people—in their arts and songs and dances. Under every rock of this great continent there is a trace of the Indian past. It is a marvelous heritage, which emerges like the waters of a secret spring out of the depths of this old, old land newly named America.

I will tell them, Marcia Highwater. I will try.

Number of Words: 1652 ÷ _____ Minutes Reading Time = Rate _____

I. VOCABULARY

*Match each word in column A with its meaning in column B.
Write the letter in the space provided.*

	A		B
_____ **1.**	dispassionate	**a.**	stared stupidly
_____ **2.**	mystified	**b.**	type of brick
_____ **3.**	gawked	**c.**	without emotion
_____ **4.**	cinderblock	**d.**	decay caused by poverty
_____ **5.**	squalor	**e.**	perplexed or bewildered

6 points for each correct answer   SCORE: _____

II. OUTLINING

*Check √ four statements below that describe how the author
outlined the selection to make the reader understand the Indian
way of life.*

_____ **1.**   He quotes what other authors have said about the
problems of Indians.

_____ **2.**   He contrasts people's way of life in Manhattan with
his mother's calm and self-confident behavior.

_____ **3.**   He describes a problem, then gives an example of
Indian wisdom that can solve it.

_____ **4.**   He describes in detail the differences between life on
an Indian reservation and life in a big city.

_____ **5.**   He describes events in his life and how they affected
his identity as an Indian.

_____ **6.**   He relates the importance of Indian values to the
survival of modern society.

_____ **7.**   He gives insights into his mother's thinking.

10 points for each correct answer   SCORE: _____

III. STORY ELEMENTS

The story makes us admire the dignity of Marcia Highwater (and therefore of Indians in general). Check √ six statements below that describe how the author shows this dignity.

_____ 1.   He shows her gentleness in helping him with his problems.

_____ 2.   He tells us that she is a stiff, moralistic person.

_____ 3.   He quotes some of her sayings, which reveal how she sees the world.

_____ 4.   He brings to life her love for the Indian way of life.

_____ 5.   He gives examples of how she is able to know what other people are thinking.

_____ 6.   He shows how she quietly settles conflicts between her children.

_____ 7.   He shows how she tries to make everyone understand her.

_____ 8.   He implies that she ignores people who stare at her.

5 points for each correct answer   SCORE: _____

PERFECT TOTAL SCORE: 100   TOTAL SCORE: _____

IV. QUESTIONS FOR THOUGHT

How has the story helped you better understand the Indian way of life? What attitudes and values of Indians do you most appreciate? Why?

Emperor of the Frozen Waste

Franklin Russell

The giant emperor penguin stood on an ice floe, facing the red midnight sun. In the cold Antarctic summer, the January sun dropped, and within 30 minutes it had risen again. The emperor balanced his 3½-foot (107-centimeter)-high body on powerfully clawed feet and dived.

Underwater, he plunged fishlike into the gloomy depths. Faster than most fish, he would stay underwater, hunting, for 20 minutes. A man would die in a matter of seconds in this frigid water. But the penguin was insulated by a layer of air trapped under his tight, oily feathers.

He would hunt and feed in these waters until the end of summer. Then, fat and strong, he would make the difficult journey to his mate, staying to help care for his offspring.

Now he headed for the surface. The water shimmered as he drove himself three feet into the air and flopped, belly down, on the ice. Hundreds of other emperors left the water with him. They stood upright— a congregation of headwaiters

in white boiled shirts and black tailcoats. The big emperor, at 100 pounds (45 kilograms) was the largest bird among them.

Here was one of the more extraordinary creatures of earth. Here was a bird who could not fly but who could, with his strong wings, swim across thousands of miles of the open sea. Here was a creature for whom the worst cold, the strongest winds, held no fears. His species had developed extraordinary abilities to combat the coming winter. They could draw on their excess fat and live for weeks, even months, without eating. Huddling together for mutual warmth, they could, with their dense feathers, survive hurricane-force winds that few other creatures could endure.

The big emperor dived again. He heard the whistling cries, grunts and gasps of whales and seals fishing the same waters. All worked hard to live in this hostile world of ice and cold. The summer months of January and February were the best hunting time of the year, and the emperor continued to feed hungrily on squid and small fish, growing ever more fat.

As fall came at the end of February, more powerful storms swept sea and ice. At

that time the big emperor stopped feeding and began walking south, with thousands of his fellow penguins falling in behind him. The migration to the ancient breeding area had begun. Each year, instinct drove them back to the same low hollow of ice.

He had made this journey six times in his eight years of life. One year the rookery lay within a mile of open water. Another year, the big emperor had walked over 25 miles (40 kilometers) of ice to reach it. This year, the ice had broken up in early February, then refrozen into upthrust masses that formed barriers. He stopped at a big chunk of ice, and the birds behind him stumbled into one another, squabbling, jostling and crying out in rage until all were halted.

After half a day, the big emperor finally scrambled over the last jagged barrier. He sped away on his belly across clear flat ice, sliding himself along with kicks of his powerful feet. Within an hour, he had reached the rookery. There he called again and again, blasting out trumpet cries to signal his mate of last year. He would recognize her with the help of her song. Each day, many females sang in front of him. Some fought among themselves for his attention, but he ignored them. He waited and walked slowly among a growing chorus of cackling, singing, courting penguins.

The temperature dropped. Soon the sun would barely rise above the northern horizon. Then would come 7 hours of pale daylight, 17 hours of night. The sea had frozen steadily, and now open water was more than 40 miles (64 kilometers) away to the north.

One evening in a savage gale he came upon a lone female standing in the shelter of a block of ice. He sang, then so did she. The big emperor

bowed, expanded his neck and sang again. He and his old mate stood close, their breasts pressing together. A grumbling roar from a splitting iceberg came to them in the wind.

That night the temperature went down to 40° below zero (-72° Celsius), and the penguins formed themselves into long, oval-shaped masses. The big emperor and his mate were packed in among thousands of other birds. The wind raged all night, but they were warm together.

The courtship of the penguins went on during April and early May, through the worst of the early-winter storms. Then silence enveloped the colony. The days grew shorter still. By the middle of May, the sun appeared above the horizon for only a few minutes; the nights became 23 hours long. One day, shortly before dawn, the female laid her egg. The big emperor joined her in a joyful duet. Around them, other pairs were singing in celebration of newly laid eggs.

The triumph of the egg, however, marked a temporary end of the betrothal of the big emperor and his mate. Soon after laying, she bowed to him and revealed the egg. The emperor sang and bowed, touching the egg with his beak. She stepped backward. The egg lay exposed on the ice.

The emperor shuffled forward and drew the egg back with his beak so it lay on top of his flat, webbed feet. He doubled his powerful claws under his feet so that the egg was lifted from the ice. Then he closed the egg into his incubating pouch. The female sang, bowed and turned away. She joined the other females headed north for open water.

During the next month, the big emperor, guarding his egg, suffered the worst of the Antarctic winter. Some of the weaker male penguins lost the will to live. When the wind blew them down, they were rolled away across the ice. Other males abandoned their eggs in the almost constant darkness and headed north for the ocean. Their eggs were often taken over by bachelor males.

Then one day a spark of light touched the northern horizon for a moment, as the tip of the sun showed above the ice. The mood of the rookery became electric. The first eggs were hatching. Chicks screamed in hunger, but it was of no use. The food-laden females were still struggling toward the rookery across more than 70 miles (113 kilometers) of ice.

In the middle of July, the big emperor felt his own egg stirring. He bent down and opened his incubating pouch to reveal the cracked egg, now jiggling violently. He closed the pouch and waited. At dawn the next day the egg broke. The tiny creature cried out and sprang from under the emperor's belly. The emperor bent down and fed the chick a small bit of milky secretion—the last of his reserves from the hunting months before. The chick's sur-

slides through the snow. The big emperor, who had been incubating nearly 65 days and had lost more than 40 pounds (18 kilograms), finally heard a familiar song. He sang back, and his mate answered.

But he could not easily give up the chick, even to her. On the second day, she attacked him with sharp blows of her beak. The chick screamed, fell out of the incubating pouch and sprawled on the ice. Both birds tried to get it back. A bachelor male then tried to steal the chick. When the confusion was over, the female had the chick in her pouch. She fed it some half-digested squid. The emperor hesitated for 24 hours, then left for the sea.

While the big emperor feasted in the spring awakening of the sea, the female carefully doled out to the chick the food she had brought back inside her body. In late August the big emperor, fat and sleek again, returned. The worst storms had passed, and the chick would now grow quickly, tended by both parents. By the end of October, when the sea ice had retreated to within a mile of the rookery, he was ready to begin hunting for himself. One morning his mother left for the sea. The big emperor stayed on and

vival depended on warmth, the tiny amount of food from its father and the remaining yolk in its own stomach. The emperor preened the chick's feathers and pushed it into his brood pouch. Now he must hang on, hungry himself, until his mate brought him relief.

The females began appearing at the end of a blizzard a week later. Fat and sleek, they walked forward as a loud cackling spread throughout the rookery. Penguins kicked themselves in tobogganing

fed the chick irregularly. One day the chick, too, was gone. He would learn instinctively to fend for himelf.

The rookery, now a long, oval-shaped, yellowish stain of pockmarked ice, started to break up in November. Ice floes crackled, groaned and split in explosive splashes of water. The big emperor stood on a floe with a group of comrades. He raised his flippers, swelled his neck and uttered his great bugling cry, as though in anticipation of the brief, rich summer of hunting in the open sea. Then, as the gloom grew, he disappeared into the bountiful Antarctic Ocean.

Number of Words: 1559 ÷ _____ Minutes Reading Time = Rate _____

I. MAIN IDEA

Check √ one statement below that best describes what the selection is about.

_____ **1.** During the breeding season, male emperor penguins raise their chicks by themselves: because they are bigger and stronger, they take the eggs away from the females.

_____ **2.** Emperor penguins have found ways to cope with a very harsh environment: their bodies, their breeding habits and their ways of raising chicks enable them to live in frigid weather.

_____ **3.** The life of an emperor penguin is so difficult that many die before they are fully grown: the cold and the lack of food kill most of them.

_____ **4.** The courtship and mating of penguins goes on during April and May, when the weather is good.

20 points for each correct answer   SCORE: _____

II. FACT/OPINION

Some of the statements below express facts; others express opinions, which may or may not be true. Write F for each sentence that is fact and O for each opinion.

_____ **1.** An emperor penguin can stay underwater for up to 20 minutes.

_____ **2.** On the ice, an emperor can move faster by sliding on his belly than by walking.

_____ **3.** With their black-and-white feathers, emperors look like headwaiters.

_____ **4.** Each year emperor penguins return to the same area to breed.

_____ **5.** When a female lays her egg, both emperor parents dance to show how happy they are.

_____ **6.** The emperor penguin's ability to survive the cold makes him the most robust creature alive.

5 points for each correct answer   SCORE: _____

III. CHARACTERIZATION

The information about emperor penguins given in the selection reveals a great deal about their "character." Match each "characteristic" listed in column A with the factual statement in column B that corresponds.

<table>
<tr><td colspan="2" align="center">A</td><td colspan="2">B</td></tr>
<tr><td>_____ **1.**</td><td>faithful</td><td>**a.**</td><td>They can survive raging storms.</td></tr>
<tr><td>_____ **2.**</td><td>devoted parents</td><td>**b.**</td><td>They have found a way to live in a hostile environment.</td></tr>
<tr><td>_____ **3.**</td><td>patient</td><td>**c.**</td><td>They can wait a long time for their mates to return from hunting.</td></tr>
<tr><td>_____ **4.**</td><td>strong</td><td>**d.**</td><td>They both look after their young.</td></tr>
<tr><td>_____ **5.**</td><td>adaptable</td><td>**e.**</td><td>They have the same mates each year.</td></tr>
</table>

10 points for each correct answer   SCORE: _____

PERFECT TOTAL SCORE: 100   TOTAL SCORE: _____

IV. QUESTIONS FOR THOUGHT

In what ways is the lifestyle of the emperor penguin similar to that of human beings? In what ways is it different?

Flying in the Face

Virginia Kraft

Not long ago a single-engine airplane took off from Mérida, Mexico, and headed across the Gulf of Mexico for the Florida Keys. Through an error, Mexican authorities did not file the plane's flight plan, and the plane turned up on U.S. radar as an unidentified aircraft approaching Cuba. Military jets were sent out to identify the plane and escort it to Key West. A line of police surrounded the plane even before it came to a stop. As its door opened, one officer turned to another and said, "Will you get a look at the pilot! She's a little old lady!"

Marion Rice Hart, the pilot, is indeed a little old lady. But although she is in her eighties, she cringes at that description almost as much as she does when she is called "Widow Hart" or a "flying grandmother." She is quick to point out that she is neither. While she

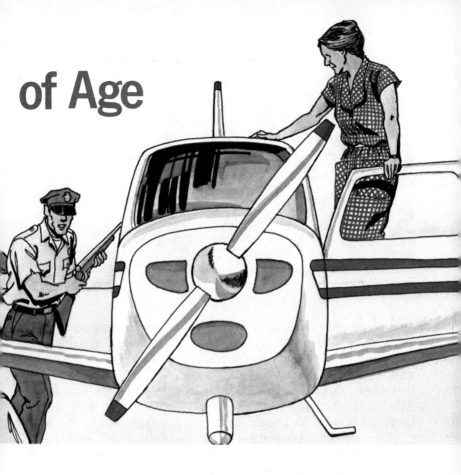

# of Age

has no objections to motherhood or grandmotherhood, she has never been a mother or a grandmother, and she was divorced, not widowed, from a man named Hart. She *did* object to his asking her why she could not act like other women.

"Now, instead of being asked why I don't act like other women," she says, "people are always asking why I don't act my age. What has age to do with the way people act? I have no idea what other people my age are doing. I don't know any."

The truth is that Marion Hart has *never* acted her age, or like other women, and she does not intend to change the habits of a lifetime. She has been a geologist, physicist, chemical engineer, artist, author, sculptor, surveyor, sailor and shortwave operator. She has worked in a copper mine in Arizona, and has been a radio operator on a B-17. She has run a locomotive

on the Southern Pacific and captained a 72-foot (22-meter) sailboat to the Indian Ocean and beyond. She has also flown her own plane across the Atlantic seven times. Her solo landings in such far places as Ceylon, Nepal, Jordan and Kuwait caused almost as much surprise as her unexpected appearance on military radar. But as far as she is concerned, the flights were very ordinary.

There is little ordinary about Marion Hart. Nothing about her strong, self-assured voice, her lean, athletic appearance, or her intent gaze suggests that she is in her eighties. In her Washington, D.C., apartment, she sits in front of a map of her wanderings. Her feet, in tennis shoes patched with pieces of old inner tubes, are propped up on a coffee table. The table is covered with navigational charts and flight manuals. Seeing her, one realizes that the idea of offering to help her across the street is as foolish as offering to drive A.J. Foyt, the champion auto racer, home. Marion Hart may be little, old and a woman, but there the comparisons end.

"I was brought up to believe what you *did* mattered, not what you didn't," she says. "I am doing today what I have always done, which is what I want to do. There's nothing unusual about that."

Marion was the fourth of six children, and one of the amazing things about the family was that at an early age every one of the kids chose a life-style. Each was intelligent and curious, and the father had the money to pay for the education they wanted.

Of the six children, Marion read the most. At 15 she came upon a magazine account of the railroad that was being built across the Andes Mountains in South America, and she decided she wanted to be an engineer. At 16 she entered Barnard College in New York City, where she stayed for two years before changing to the Massachusetts Institute of Technology. There her interest in railroads gave way to an interest in chemistry. In 1913 she became the first woman to receive a chemical engineering degree from M.I.T.—or, as far as anyone knows, from anywhere else.

She worked for a while, then went back to school and got a master's degree in geology. This led to marriage and the mining camp in Arizona. After her divorce, Marion Rice Hart continued to study and write about the many things that interested her.

One thing, however, that never interested her was clothes. She said they only complicated her life, so she has designed a dress for all seasons. It is shapeless, sacklike, drip-dry, with huge zippered pockets for carrying passports and flight manuals. When she needs one, she has it made up wherever she happens to be. Her sneakers are always worn until they are old and threadbare, and she has been known to sew large buttons over holes in the toes.

Those who know her well say she has a tough streak of self-discipline and great determination. But she has never had any interest in setting marks or breaking records, only in learning new things and learning them well.

Marion Rice Hart taking time from a busy flying schedule to pose beside her single engine airplane

When she wanted to learn to fly, she had trouble finding someone to teach her. This was after World War II, and the instructors who were available were not much interested in teaching a woman. She tried several, but all of them treated her like a cranky lady. No doubt she gave them a hard time, for she is not the type to be shown how without also being told why. Since she probably knew more, in theory, about flight than they did, her endless questions must have driven them to quit.

She does her own navigation when she flies, as she does when she sails. She has, in fact, written a book on navigation, *How to Navigate Today.* It is still considered an outstanding manual for small-boat sailors and beginning fliers.

Marion has spent little time on the ground since taking to the air. She has flown over almost every square mile of the United States, over much of South and Central America, Europe and Africa. In the early years she made the ocean crossings with copilots, but after she made her first successful solo crossing at 74, she decided she had no future need for copilots. "They just take up room," she says. "If you have a copilot who is a better pilot than you, then you are just a passenger, and if he is not as good as you, then he is just a nuisance. If the plane is already overloaded, there is no reason to add another 160 pounds (73 kilograms) to it."

She often refuses to carry a life raft, although officials repeatedly insist that she must. "Flying across the North Atlantic, the water is 37° Fahrenheit (3° Celsius)," she says. "How long will you last sitting in a rubber tub?"

She prefers to carry her extra weight in gasoline. She does, however, carry a survival kit of sorts. It consists of a Boy Scout hunting knife, a quart canteen of water, a flashlight and a book of matches.

It is not Marion Hart's nature to worry. "I can't say I was ever so frightened I was hysterical," she says, "but things happen. A bird flew into a wing and ripped it open in Ethiopia. On my first plane the main spar that holds the wings on cracked in flight. Fortunately, the wings did not fall off until I was on the ground. I had two radios on the trip last year and lost both of them. Before I managed to get where I was going by dead reckoning, I flew

through a military zone closed to air traffic.

"Then, coming into Iceland my communications receiver went bad. At the same time the Iceland beacon went off the air. I did not know whether the beacon, my radio, or what, was out. When I passed the weather ship, they told me I was on a course I did not expect to be on. I decided my compass must be faulty. I reached up and felt a drop of compass fluid. But I had eight hours of gas left, so I could not very well declare an emergency. I just kept going, and, fortunately, Iceland turned up.

"People always ask me about close calls," she says. "My answer to that is 'nothing fatal.'"

She is even more positive when asked about being lost. "I have never been lost," she snaps, "only mislaid."

It is difficult to imagine Marion Rice Hart being lost or mislaid anywhere, but it is even more difficult to imagine her ever slowing down. Age, after all, is for old people, and Marion Hart has had more than 80 years of experience in staying young and active.

Number of Words: 1438 ÷ _____ Minutes Reading Time = Rate _____

I. INFERENCES

Check ✓ five statements below that can be inferred from the selection.

_____ **1.** A person can have more than one career in life and be successful in all of them.

_____ **2.** Marion Rice Hart is a determined person because she comes from a large family.

_____ **3.** Being old does not mean that people must stop doing what interests them.

_____ **4.** Only people who are as independent and tough-minded as Marion Rice Hart can be successful.

_____ **5.** A person should not stop trying to do something just because there are difficulties along the way.

_____ **6.** There is no reason a woman can't do hard work, such as running a locomotive or sailing a boat.

_____ **7.** If people see themselves as capable of success, often they will succeed.

6 points for each correct answer   SCORE: _____

II. CRITICAL THINKING

Circle the letter (a, b or c) of each correct answer below.

1. What does the author feel toward Marion Hart?
a. resentment   **b.** admiration   **c.** sympathy

2. How does the author make Marion Hart believable?
a. by showing her strengths and weaknesses
b. by showing only her strengths
c. by showing only her weaknesses

3. What quality does the author most admire in Marion Hart?
a. her courage   **b.** her strength   **c.** her pride

4. Marion Hart's thinking might best be described as
   a. reactionary   **b.** independent   **c.** radical

5. Marion Hart's life serves as an inspiration to
   a. the very young
   b. the very old
   c. young and old

8 points for each correct answer   SCORE: _____

III. PROBLEM SOLVING

The story mentions that, while flying an airplane, Marion Rice Hart has "never been lost, only mislaid." Check √ five actions below that could help a pilot find his or her way at night without a compass.

_____ **1.** fly around in circles, trying to figure out where he or she is

_____ **2.** try to navigate by the stars

_____ **3.** try to locate a light beacon from a harbor or airport

_____ **4.** use maps and knowledge of direction and speed

_____ **5.** try to contact a weather ship by radio

_____ **6.** try to go back to where he or she took off

_____ **7.** use the radio

6 points for each correct answer   SCORE: _____

PERFECT TOTAL SCORE: 100   TOTAL SCORE: _____

IV. QUESTIONS FOR THOUGHT

Are there any lessons you can learn from the story of Marion Rice Hart that can apply to you? What are they? Explain.

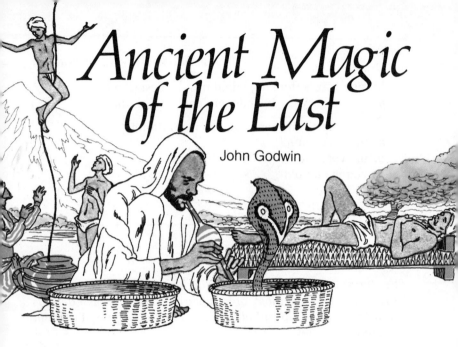

Ancient Magic of the East

John Godwin

There are in this astounding land wizards who can make serpents dance to the flute, while others will cause a tree to grow before your very eyes. Others still can cast a spell upon a length of rope so that it stands upright like a candle in the empty air. Some will also permit themselves to be entombed beneath the ground, remaining thus buried for a great period of time and yet emerge again hale in body and spirit. Such men will also take their ease reclining upon boards studded with sharp nails. . . . And then there are those who are able to walk on flames and yet do not burn. . . .

The above is from a letter written in 1703 by James Buckfield, junior clerk of the East India Company, to his sister in England. Chances are that Mr. Buckfield never really saw more than one or two of the marvels about which he wrote to his sister. The rest he probably knew only from hearsay. But his letter is interesting because it is the first record to list almost the whole bag of tricks that came to be known as the magic of the Orient, or East.

The first Europeans who saw or heard about these wonders of the East considered them magic because they could find no reasonable explanation for them. They did not even distinguish between the two different kinds of acts. There were those performed by sleight-of-hand entertainers, often based on trickery and the idea that the hand can be quicker than the eye. There were also those performed by genuine *fakirs*, or spiritual ascetics, which demonstrated the power of mind over body.

SNAKE CHARMING

The first Eastern trick to arouse European wonder—and still the most popular—was snake charming. A poisonous snake is made to dance—that is, sway back and forth—to the tune of a flute. The snake is supposed to become so entranced by the snake charmer's music that it "gets rhythm" and forgets to bite.

Now it so happens that snakes are stone-deaf. They pick up sound vibrations from the ground, but they can't hear anything transmitted by air. The only purpose of the flute is to attract a crowd.

The snake is always defanged. No snake charmer in his right mind would face a snake still in possession of its weapon. The defanged snake

Sinhalese snake charmers attract customers with flute and "dancing" snake.

will not bite because its mouth is sore. Nonetheless, instinctively it will still spar for a striking position. And therein lies all the mystery of snake charming. As the performer raises the lid of the snake basket, he kicks the side, and the snake rears up. Then, while blowing his gourd pipe, the charmer sways his body from side to side, and the snake follows his movements—just as it would even if the charmer weren't playing anything at all. The moment the performer stops swaying, the snake does the same. Snake charmers usually perform with cobras because they are more sluggish than the faster moving kraits and vipers.

Snake charming is practiced from Morocco to Thailand, and is always performed with defanged creatures.

THE "GROWING TREE TRICK"

The "Growing Tree Trick"—also known as the "Mango Miracle"—originated in India. When Western magicians copied it, the stunt became unfashionable in its country of origin.

This spectacular trick can be done only with a mango. It takes half an hour or more to perform. The people watching see the magician squat down and plant in the ground a mango pit the size of a large chestnut. He then sets up a tripod of three long sticks over the spot. He elaborately covers this with his cloak, forming a rough tent. After repeating prayers over it, the magician whips away the cloak and reveals a little green shoot pushing out of the ground. The cloak goes back; more prayers follow; and next time there is a tiny tree growing under the tripod. Finally, after yet more prayers, the cloak is removed once again. And behold—there is a 2-foot (0.6-meter)-high mango tree, complete with several fruits, which the magician picks and hands to the audience to eat.

This trick is impressive but surprisingly simple once you know how it's done. Like every other good piece of stage magic, this trick requires a lot of practice and a good spiel. The success of the act depends on the dexterity of the performer and the rubber-like qualities of the mango plant. This particular plant can be rolled up into a small space, and it will, when released, snap back to full size without damage. The first little sprig is coiled up inside the hollow mango pit. As the magician sets up the tent, he breaks the thin shell, and the sprig "grows" from the ground.

All the other growth stages are hidden in various pockets of the cloak and are planted into the earth each time the magician rearranges the tent. The prayers only serve to build suspense and to strengthen the illusion of a growing process.

THE INDIAN ROPE TRICK

But the most outstanding of all these Indian tricks has always been the Indian rope trick, which is claimed to be more than 700 years old. The first European credited with mentioning the rope trick was Marco Polo, who reported that he witnessed a performance of it at the court of the Mongol ruler Kublai Khan in 1289. Some Indian sources believe that the trick originated in China, and was brought to India by a troupe of Tartar jugglers.

Wherever its birthplace, the great rope trick has become an Indian tradition. Almost as soon as the British went to India, they began to send home accounts of this trick, usually without having witnessed it. One of the several versions about which they reported goes as follows:

The magician takes a piece of rope about 40 feet (12 meters) long and throws it into the air. Two, three, four times it flops back to the ground as any rope would. But the fifth—or tenth—time it remains absolutely rigid, rearing high above

Magicians performing popular Indian rope trick

while the magician motions at it from below.

Then the magician calls his apprentice, a small boy, and orders him to climb up the rope. The boy is not willing and says that he is tired. The magician, angry at this disobedience, grabs a stick and chases the boy up the rope. From above, the boy lets fly with some juicy insults. Enraged, the magician pulls out a huge dagger, shakes his fist at the boy, and proceeds to climb up the rope after him. At the top, there is a confused struggle, a few screams, and down falls what appears to be the boy's lifeless body.

The magician comes down, waving his dagger. His assistants, weeping and frightened, place the boy's body in a box. The magician slams the lid of the box shut, closes his eyes, murmurs a long incantation and gives the box a hearty kick. Whereupon, the lid flies open, and out climbs the boy, grinning and in excellent health and humor. He proves this by running around the audience collecting money.

As the term indicates, the rope trick is a trick. It needs a prepared setting, a boy both very small and well trained, at least four other assistants, and

a magician of outstanding skill and agility.

The first thing necessary for the act is the right location. It has to be staged either in a built-up area or on a hilly landscape. Before the audience gathers, a thin but strong wire is stretched overhead between two high points, rooftops or hilltops. The trick is always performed at dusk and always accompanied by the lighting of bonfires. It appears that the fires are to attract attention. Their real purpose is to add an uneven flicker to the already dim light, making the wire, high above the ground, quite invisible.

The magician's 40-foot (12-meter) rope has tiny grappling hooks concealed at one end. He throws it up until the hooks catch the wire, making the rope appear to stand, whereas it actually hangs. The illusion is helped because the attention of the audience is focused on the rope, so they do not notice the supporting wire.

When the magician pursues his apprentice up the rope, he is wearing a full cloak. Concealed underneath it is the fake body. Strapped to the magician's body is a kind of leather harness. He catches the boy at the top of the rope, where the spectators can see only hazily. He and the boy struggle; the boy screams; and the magician drops what appears to be the boy's body, causing the audience to look at the ground. Unwatched, the boy quickly climbs into the harness and is carried down, hidden beneath the magician's cloak.

When the fake body is put into the box, the magician looks inside, keeping the open lid between himself and the audience. Covered by the lid, the boy climbs out of the harness and into the box. A minute later, the surprised viewers see the boy come out unharmed. The magician motions again, his assistants cut the wire, and the rope drops. The great trick is accomplished.

Some Western observers can see no special distinction between a fakir lying on a bed of nails and a snake charmer working his cobra. But in fact these two performances belong to quite different categories. The habit of lumping them together instead of considering them individually is responsible for much confusion.

The snake charmers and tree growers are professional entertainers, like the stage magician with his top hat full of rabbits. These men perform tricks and lay no claim to be doing anything else. But the fakir does not intend to "entertain." By reclining on a nail-studded board or by causing himself other physical discomforts, the fakir is demonstrating the dom-

inance of his spirit over his body.

The government of India takes a rather dim view of these practices. Over the past 20 years, the government has banned most of these exercises. Nevertheless the self-torture goes on, because this is the way some of these spiritual men earn their living. There are, of course, thousands of hermits, who meditate, fast and suffer in the solititude of mountain peaks or forests. But many of these holy men seem to prefer an audience that gives money and admiration. In either case the enduring of pain is real enough—real, though not quite as horrifying as it appears.

If you press your hand down on a single nail sticking from a board, the result will be a nasty puncture. Do the same on a board closely studded with nails and you would not get a scratch. If they are dense enough, the nails will offer an almost solid surface. This is the principle of the fakir's nail bed, which is as closely studded as a hairbrush, and therefore allows him to stretch out on it with some discomfort but with no injury.

No other performers have equaled the fakir's body control, although several West-

The famous Houdini about to perform a feat of mind over body

erners—notably Harry Houdini—have managed incredible performances. The secret behind these feats is the mind-over-matter formula. Human willpower can influence physical functions more than we used to believe possible. Since the recent interest in yoga, the Western world has become more familiar with this fact, but we still have only an inkling of the extent to which this phenomenon is true.

A fakir, willing to give up a normal life and to concentrate for years on his brain-body relationship to the exclusion of everything else, can achieve control that appears miraculous. He is able to regulate the blinking of his eyelids, develop dexterity in his toes equal to that of his fingers and tense or relax almost any muscle at will. Some can slow down or speed up pulse beat and contract certain muscles that will cause blood circulation to come almost to a standstill.

Several years ago, three Indian yogis underwent tests prepared by the University of Michigan Medical School. Each of the three could reduce his heartbeat until it could not be heard through a stethoscope. Fifty years earlier, medical science would have pronounced these men dead.

There are stories in Indian folklore of religious men who let themselves be buried for 10 and even 50 years. According to the stories, they were found to be not only alive but minus a beard. Supposedly, they were able to suspend hair growth along with all other bodily functions. In the 1920s and 30s, American magazines regularly printed these yarns, but did not mention that educated Indians regarded the stories in roughly the same light as we regard the tale of Rip Van Winkle.

Harry Houdini once staged a burial act of his own under circumstances that allowed no trickery of any kind. He had himself locked in a watertight metal box that was lowered to the bottom of a swimming pool. There the box remained, clearly visible to hundreds of people, for one hour and 28 minutes before Houdini pulled the signal cord. He came out feeling faint and nauseated but otherwise unharmed, and he was soon able to give an account of his experience.

Houdini had mastered the art of breath control as thoroughly as any Eastern fakir. He found it quite unnecessary to go into a trance. By remaining perfectly still and keeping his breathing down to a minimum, Houdini performed a feat most doctors would have considered impossible. Houdini, in fact, could duplicate almost any fakir feat without the trance. But even the great Houdini never attempted fire walking.

FIRE WALKING

Fire walking is practiced in many places, as well as India. Only in India is it regarded as a religious rite. In other places people consider it a form of entertainment. The one feature shared by all fire walkers is the complete mystery that surrounds the art. Of all the

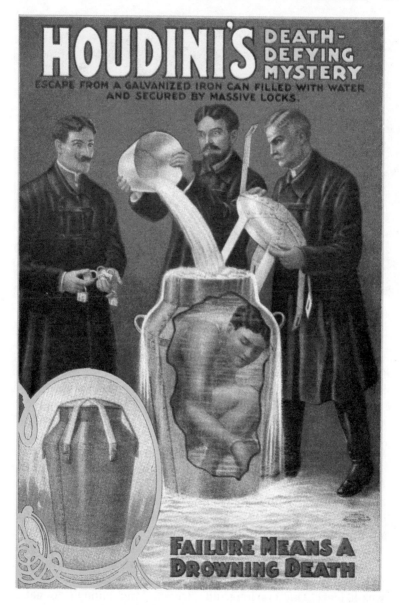

One of many posters, typical of the 20s, advertising popular Houdini show

Fire walker crosses fire pit as crowds look on.

world's many exotic puzzles, fire walking remains the most baffling.

In 1959 I watched a fire-walking ceremony on Bora Bora, an island in the South Pacific. The event was announced several days beforehand, like a circus performance. People gathered from every part of the little isle in what was like a family picnic atmosphere.

By the time I arrived, the firepit was going full blast. It was 40 feet (12 meters) long and about half as wide. I couldn't estimate the depth because the heat near the edge was almost unbearable. The heat came from large rocks that had been lying on a bed of burning logs and charcoal for the past 48 hours. Now the rocks were glowing red-hot, making the air above the pit shimmer with the kind of heat waves you see around a blast furnace.

Aside from several hundred islanders, there were three French naval officers and one policeman. Several of us tried to stand at the edge of the trench long enough to get a good look, but the glow was enough to singe our eyebrows.

Fire walking remains a popular entertainment for visitors to India.

In spite of our sunglasses, the blowtorch effect on our faces became agonizing within seconds. The attendants obliged us by dropping a few colored rags into the pit. There was a momentary flicker of flame, and the rags turned to powder.

At three o'clock sharp, the fire walkers appeared. There were eight of them, all handsome, athletic young Tahitians, looking like figures straight off a travel poster. Their arrival was quite unceremonious. They mingled with the tourists, answered questions in broken French and grinned boyishly

when we inspected their feet for possible protective coatings. Their soles were hard and tough, but no more so than those of anyone who is accustomed to going barefoot.

Then a patter of drums sounded, and the eight men formed a single line and picked up palm branches. They began to sing one of the melodious island chants and, eyes straight ahead, marched toward the pit. At the edge, the leader struck the ground in front of him with his branch.

Then he walked into the trench, just as calmly as he

might step into a wading pool. The haze of heat blurred his figure, and I tensed myself for a scream of agony and the sizzle of burning flesh. He kept going, stepping gingerly over the uneven rocks but nevertheless striding along nonchalantly. Halfway through the length of the pit, he raised his palm branch as a signal. One by one, the other seven men followed him, walking with the same sure-footed stride.

They filed out at the other end of the pit, rested for a few moments, then resumed their single file formation for the return trip. This time they followed close behind their leader, and they seemed to progress a little faster.

Each of the walks across the fiery pit was accompanied by the tapping of drums, which beat steadily until the last of the walkers had completed his round.

The eight men were breathing deeply after their walk. I noticed that their bodies were drenched in sweat. The soles of their feet were black with charcoal, yet the skin under the charcoal was quite unharmed. A couple of men had developed a few little blisters around their ankles, but no more than this. As a matter of fact, their feet felt cooler to me than the rest of their bodies.

Later, I asked the policeman if he had seen many of these ceremonies. He said, yes, about eight or nine. And all exactly like the one we had seen? Yes.

"How do you think it's done?" I asked.

He gave a shrug. "Who knows? They just do it."

This answer pretty well sums up our knowledge on the subject, although fire walkers have never shown reluctance to have their ceremony observed, filmed and investigated. Some few inquiring scientists have actually participated in these rites. Several came out of the ordeal without a blister; others were badly burned at the first step. How do they account for the different results? They don't.

Number of Words: 2993 ÷ _____ Minutes Reading Time = Rate _____

I. FACT/OPINION

Write F for each sentence that states a fact. Write O for each sentence that states an opinion.

_____ **1.** There are wizards who can cast a spell upon a length of rope so that it stands upright like a candle in the air.

_____ **2.** Snakes are stone-deaf; they pick up sound vibrations from the ground but can't hear anything transmitted by air.

_____ **3.** The "Growing Tree" trick is impressive but surprisingly simple once you know how it's done.

_____ **4.** By reclining on a rail-studded board, the fakir proves the dominance of his spirit over his body.

_____ **5.** The feet of the fire walkers seemed cooler than the rest of their bodies.

6 points for each correct answer   SCORE: _____

II. SUPPORTING DETAILS

Complete each of the phrases below in column A by writing the letter of the answer from column B.

	A		B
_____ **1.**	Snake charming	**a.**	is a trick done with a mango.
_____ **2.**	"Tree Growing"		
_____ **3.**	Lying on a bed of nails	**b.**	remains a mystery.
		c.	seems to need music.
_____ **4.**	Controlling one's heartbeat	**d.**	may cause discomfort but no injury.
_____ **5.**	Fire walking	**e.**	requires great concentration.

6 points for each correct answer   SCORE: _____

III. SUMMARY

Check √ four statements that would be included in a short summary of the selection.

_____ **1.** For a long time, Europeans have been curious about amazing feats of magic performed by people in the East.

_____ **2.** The fact that many people are still taken in by these feats shows how ignorant they are.

_____ **3.** Some of these feats are based on tricks and illusions, while others are serious demonstrations of control over one's body.

_____ **4.** There is a logical explanation for all these feats, except the fire-walking performance.

_____ **5.** The people who perform the fire-walking act are either in a trance or cover their bodies with special creams.

_____ **6.** People in many parts of the world perform the fire-walking act without suffering any burns.

10 points for each correct answer   SCORE: _____

PERFECT TOTAL SCORE: 100   TOTAL SCORE: _____

IV. QUESTIONS FOR THOUGHT

What ideas has the selection introduced to you? What is so attractive about magic? Explain.

Starter for Success

Joseph Mastrangello

The starter's pistol cracks. The runners in the women's mile relay break from the starting blocks, heads high, legs moving in swift rhythm. Gail Fitzgerald of the Brooklyn Atoms takes the baton and tears into the lead. From now on the other runners will see only the backs of the blue-clad Brooklyn girls as they widen the lead and win the race by 40 yards (37 meters). The public-address system booms: "Winner, women's mile relay, Brooklyn Atoms Track Club. Time 3:45.7. A new world's record."

The four Atoms joyfully hug their coach. "You said we'd do it," they shout. "Oh, Freddie, thank you, thank you." Fred Thompson takes a white handkerchief from his pocket and blows his nose, hoping to hide the tears of pride. Then quickly he becomes the coach again, issuing orders. "Okay, get into your sweat suits, move around, don't tighten up."

In 18 years, scenes like this have become almost commonplace. The Brooklyn Atoms have set dozens of records and won impressive medals and trophies. These girls, who might never have left the trash-littered streets and aimless life of the neighborhood they came from, have represented the United States in the Munich and Montreal Olympic Games. Undoubtedly they will represent the United States at the next Olympic Games.

The trophies and medals are only a part of the story. Far more important are the lives that have been saved. Thirteen-, fourteen-, fifteen-year-old girls who might have grown up as dropouts or addicts have become, instead, productive young women. Coach Thompson ticks off the numbers: Shelly Marshall, 3.9; Cheryl Toussaint, 3.7; Denise Hooten, 3.8. These are not track records, but the college grade-point averages (out of a possible 4) of some famous members of the Brooklyn Atoms.

"Winning races and setting records is fine," says Thompson. "But I would much rather go to a college graduation and see one of these kids receive her diploma. That's what this is all about."

Fred Thompson grew up in the Bedford-Stuyvesant section of Brooklyn in New York City. In this section are many blocks of grimy brownstones and burned-out buildings. Unemployed men stand listlessly in front of abandoned stores;

Residents walking the streets at night in a downtown section of Brooklyn's Bedford Stuyvesant

addicts lie in hallways. Children move through this obstacle course each day on their way to school. Here crime replaces the Little League for many. Fred Thompson knew this neighborhood well.

When Thompson received his Army discharge in 1959, he returned to Bedford-Stuyvesant. He was appalled by the countless kids wandering about aimlessly. "I got bugged," Thompson says with great feeling. "I remembered the writer who said, 'You can't go home again,' but I knew I had to. I had to work with these kids."

Like many of the girls who came to him for help, Thompson came from a broken home. His parents separated when he was young. He and his brother, John, were taken into the home of a great-aunt, Ira Johnson, and her husband. The life of the streets was all around them, and the tough, colorful gangs roaming these streets seemed adventurous to young Fred. But he worked from six in the morning to six at night helping out in the small store run by his aunt and uncle. Fortunately this left him too tired at night to join a gang or to get into trouble.

Two members of Atoms' track team vie with other contestants for lead in middle distance race.

Thompson graduated from City College and went to law school at St. John's University. To help pay his way through school, he worked at night and during the summers in the community centers in Brooklyn. They stressed sports there, for discipline and for burning up youthful energies.

When he became a successful attorney, Thompson still returned each night to P.S. 21, a school located in a typical district of Bedford-Stuyvesant. He set up a 60-yard (55-meter) dash in the hallway and soon had 200 kids running.

"The boys had plenty of sports available. So I phased them out of the races in 1962 and concentrated on helping the girls," Thompson recalls. "The Brooklyn Atoms were born in that school hallway. It started as a social project," he says, "and I guess it still is."

Cheryl Toussaint is typical of the girls Thompson has

helped. She was a gangling 13-year-old when she heard about a girls' track meet at the Boys High School field. She went there wearing jeans and a pair of sneakers a bit too large for her, but she had determination.

She entered the 100-yard (91-meter) dash and finished a close fourth, losing to three Atoms. Within a few years, she had become one of the top middle-distance runners in the nation. She was one of the first Atoms to make an international team and the first to bring back an Olympic silver medal to Bedford-Stuyvesant. Running in a 600-meter race in Canada in 1970, Cheryl broke the world's record, and she has an American record for the 800-meter run.

Cheryl went to New York University and majored in math, graduating with the highest honors. Then she entered a management training program at the Federal Reserve Bank. Each evening she would leave Wall Street for Bedford-Stuyvesant to work out with the Atoms. She changed in the same locker room as the younger girls, who looked at her with awe and admiration, inspired by the woman who had made it. She tells people, "Running didn't make me rich; it

Cheryl Toussaint winning 800-meter event at U.S. Olympic Invitational Track Meet in New York's Madison Square Garden

made me wealthy in spirit." Fred Thompson helped to develop that spirit.

At the Atoms' nightly training sessions, Thompson is the only authority on the field. He may be working with 5 or 25

Competitors running in single file during event at Colgate Games

girls at any practice, but they all listen raptly to that one voice.

A stopwatch hangs from his neck, as he starts the girls off in small groups. Now he is in perpetual motion as he runs across the infield to shout instructions. "Lengthen your stride, extend, extend," he yells to one as he moves along beside her. Satisfied that she is doing all right, he jogs to another section of the track to encourage another. "It's not a fight, relax and breathe, come on, keep moving."

A well-run practice makes Thompson content as he watches the girls leave the field to walk home. He always believed that track would help his girls to a better way of life, open new horizons. But he also knew that his program could not help enough girls. He looked for ways to help not dozens but thousands of girls to compete.

He found a way when he met David R. Foster, chairman of the Colgate-Palmolive-Peet Company. Foster was interested in helping Thompson to develop a program that would get a lot of women involved in sports. Together they came up with the idea for the Colgate Women's Games.

The competition would include everyone from six-year-olds to national champions and world record-holders. All girls and young women living in New York City and in Jersey City would be eligible. Scholastic grants totaling more than $25,000 a year were to be awarded. The games were to provide a training ground for inner-city girls and young women who might otherwise have no opportunity for sports.

In the first year of the Colgate Women's Games (1975), 5000 girls and young women participated. In 1978 there were more than 20,000.

The 1978 Colgate Games began with the preliminaries. On a Sunday morning in February, as New York was still digging itself out of a snowstorm, the gym at Pratt Institute in Brooklyn was a blur of movement. Five thousand girls from grades one through five competed, many for the first time in their lives. It was the second weekend of the preliminaries; they were to be run over five long weekends, with the semifinals on the sixth weekend. For those who made it, there would be the finals in Madison Square Garden on the 13th of March.

The gym at Pratt was in an uproar. So many races were being run that the crack of the starters' pistols sounded like a small war. A three-year-old broke away from her parents and took off around the track. Spectators grinned and cheered. As the child crossed the finish line, Thompson shouted, "Look at that. That's what it's all about."

As the youngsters were leaving, Thompson found a chair in a quiet place off to the side. He placed his elbows on his knees, touched his fingers together and talked about graduations he had attended.

A little competitor proudly displays sweater she has won.

"One of the most important was Shelly Marshall's. She was the first of the Atoms to make it all the way out of the ghetto to go on to graduate with honors and then to earn her master's degree. Nothing came easy to Shelly. She was gutsy and fought for everything she got. There were others, great ones, but Shelly was the first, and I knew that she was setting an example."

Fred stared out across the floor and talked about his 18 years with the Atoms and how much of his personal life he had given up. Should he quit? he wondered out loud, but a nine-year-old headed toward him with a problem. He went to meet her, listened, answered and patted her on the head. Watching her walk away, he shrugged his shoulders. "No," he said, convincing himself, "I can't desert them now."

Several weeks later, on the afternoon of March 13, the fi-

Former tennis great Althea Gibson and New York City Mayor Lindsay participating in track ceremony at Madison Square Garden

nals of the Colgate Women's Games were held at Madison Square Garden in New York City. The entrance march of the finalists had all the pomp of an Olympic opening.

Down on the floor, Cheryl Toussaint helped at the finish line. Denise Hooten, another Atom, an honor scholar at New York University and now a candidate for a master's degree in exercise physiology at Columbia University, gave her expert help to injured runners.

For a brief moment Fred Thompson stood near the edge of the arena, maybe thinking of the corridor of P.S. 21 when his girls flew around the track relaying the baton from one to the other. Maybe the baton had looked to him like a rolled-up diploma. It was exactly that for many of his girls because of his encouragement.

Thompson is well known throughout the world of track and field. But he has become a symbol to the girls who look to him for a way to get out of a life that is pressing them down. Typical is 12-year-old Dolores Smith, a member of the Atoms. She says, "I want to go to college and be a nurse or a lawyer.

Atoms coach Fred Thompson enjoying the recognition of track fans.

But I think about the 1984 Olympics a lot, especially when I'm running."

Thompson knows this, and he has spent his time and half his lifetime salary showing girls a better way of life through athletics. He will continue to work as a lawyer and to help girls like Dolores Smith. He hopes she will win medals, but he hopes even more that someday she will become Dolores Smith, Registered Nurse or Attorney-at-Law. That's what it all started out to be—a social project— and it still is.

Number of Words: 1877 ÷ _____ Minutes Reading Time = Rate _____

I. LANGUAGE USAGE

The italicized word in each sentence below has two possible pronunciations, depending upon how it is used. Indicate the correct pronunciation of the word as it is used in the sentence by writing A if the accent is on the first syllable or B if the accent is on the second syllable. Refer to columns A and B in making your choice.

_____ **1.** The Brooklyn Atoms have set dozens of *records*.

_____ **2.** A well-run practice makes Thompson *content*.

_____ **3.** I can't *desert* them now.

_____ **4.** The *entrance* march had the pomp of an Olympic opening.

_____ **5.** It started out to be a social *project* and it still is.

A	B
re´cords	re cords´
con´tent	con tent´
de´sert	de sert´
en´trance	en trance´
pro´ject	pro ject´

5 points for each correct answer   SCORE: _____

II. SKIMMING

By skimming the selection, match each person listed in column A with one of his or her achievements in column B. Write the letter for each answer in the space provided.

A	B
_____ **1.** Cheryl Toussaint	**a.** became a successful attorney.

_____ **2.** Shelly Marshall   **b.** was an honor student at New York University.

_____ **3.** Fred Thompson   **c.** helped start the Colgate Women's Games.

_____ **4.** Denise Hooten   **d.** won an Olympic silver medal.

_____ **5.** David Foster   **e.** was the first Atom to get a master's degree.

5 points for each correct answer   SCORE: _____

III. SEQUENCE

Number the statements below in the order in which they happened in Fred Thompson's life.

_____ **a.** He went back to Bedford/Stuyvesant.
_____ **b.** He worked in his uncle's store.
_____ **c.** He attended law school.
_____ **d.** He set up the first race for girls in a school hallway.
_____ **e.** He saw his idea for Women's Games come true.

4 points for each correct answer   SCORE: _____

PERFECT TOTAL SCORE: 100   TOTAL SCORE: _____

IV. QUESTIONS FOR THOUGHT

Do you have a special interest you would like to develop (sports, music, photography, etc.)? How could someone like Fred Thompson help you with it?

Modern Britons Try the Iron Age

Two women out gathering spring flowers in the woods of England in 1977 were startled when they came face to face with a wild-looking man with a beard. The man wore a rough woolen tunic and carried a primitive knife. The woods were private, the stranger told them, so would they please go away and tell no one what they had seen. About the same time, woodsmen had seen long-haired people busy setting traps for squirrels or chasing rabbits with swift-running ferrets.

Three hundred years before the birth of Christ, an ancient people called *Celts* had lived in these lands. Now, from these strange goings-on, it appeared that some long-lost band of Celts had survived into the 20th century. Had they somehow been bypassed by the different groups of invaders who had swept over the island, even by modern people, until now? Well, not exactly. This "Iron Age" community was simply the brainchild of a British Broadcasting Corporation producer named John Percival. He was fed up with archeology shows on TV that showed only diggers digging and archeologists talking. He thought of a secret project to create an Iron Age village to give people a better understanding of what that life was really like. (The Iron Age in Great Britain was about 2300 years ago.)

From a thousand volunteers, he chose six couples and three children. These people would spend a year living in a careful reconstruction of an Iron Age settlement. An estate owner rented them 35 acres (14 hectares) of woods and 15 acres (6 hectares) of fields down a dead-end lane. They would be relatively cut off from all contact with the outside world. The only concession the BBC would make to the 20th century was to allow the settlers medical supplies and emergency visits by a doctor. There were also some rules imposed on them by the government. These required schoolbooks for the children and four exits from the hand-built round house to satisfy fire laws. And, of course, John Percival and his television crew came jolting through the woods in Land Rovers twice a week to film what was going on. This re-

Members of the village gather to eat—Iron Age style.

creation of Celtic life is now a 12-part TV series. (The village was to be burned after the experiment to protect the estate owner from hordes of curious tourists.)

So one chilly March day in 1977, a bold band took off their modern jeans and sweaters, donned woolen shirts handed out by the BBC and set up tents. In the group were three schoolteachers, a hairdresser, a nurse, a doctor, a social worker, a builder, a mathematician, a National Farmers Union official, two students and three children aged seven, five and three years.

All the BBC had done in advance was to clear a site in the woods, bulldoze a boundary wall of earth and hand out a few metal tools. Water had also been piped in to a "well," because the water table was 200 feet (61 meters) down. Tents were needed because the settlers would have no other shelter until they built it. For company they had a mongrel dog named Sirius and an Old English sheepdog called Emer. They also had 3 cows, 4 pigs, nine goats, 25 sheep, 40 chickens and some bees.

After the 20th-century vehicles drove away, an Iron Age calm settled over the woods.

The volunteers went to work to build a home and create such comforts as they could. But they were not entirely unprepared. They had taken evening classes in potting, metalworking and weaving. And they had been advised by "survival" experts on what safely could be eaten in the woods.

Happily, they survived. British archeologists differ over whether they have truly lived as Iron Age people. But without question they have existed much closer to the life of 2300 years ago than of today. I saw this during a visit I made just before their stay ended.

I started out for my visit in the modern comfort of an automobile. But my car sank in the muddy track long before I reached the Iron Age village, so I left it and set out on foot. After about a mile, there was a whiff of woodsmoke, and presently a clearing opened out. I saw a few goats straying about and a rather ragged figure in a woolen jerkin and trousers. He had a huge basket of logs on his back and was staggering toward a compound in the middle.

The area was surrounded by an earth wall topped by a fence. Over the gate was a sheep's head, an Iron Age sign of welcome. Within was a

Two young residents of the Celtic village tending to their chores

yard, ankle-deep in mud, through which a cheerful round-faced woman with bare feet was lugging a bucket of water from the well. A young fellow with a squirrel cap and calf-leather moccasins was sitting on a log. He was twisting and bending strips of wood into a basket. A round house dominated the scene. I had to stoop slightly to enter its deerskin door. I was at first confused by the darkness and smoke. Apart from the small doors, the only light came from the log fire blazing in the center. A big black cauldron was suspended over the flames.

The barefooted woman, whose name was Kate Rossetti, set down her water bucket and started stirring the cauldron. She was preparing a beef stew. Nearby in a clay oven, the day's bread was baking. Her husband, John, eased the basket of logs off his back and began stacking them by the fire. "We never allow it to go out," he explained, "and it eats up wood—a ton (.907 metric ton) every five days. Actually we have succeeded in making fire by rubbing two pieces of wood together, but we aren't expert."

As my eyes grew accustomed to the gloom, I remarked how large the round house was. "It's 48 feet (15 meters) across and nearly 30 feet (9 meters) high," said John, "but it took us much longer to build than we expected. We spent six weeks making the basic structure and eight weeks thatching. We worked all day, every day, on it." Straw blinds and screens divided the house into 13 "rooms" around the low walls. This gave each couple the modern luxury of some privacy. They slept between animal skins on low wooden beds.

The round house proved surprisingly warm and comfortable. Indeed, the Iron Agers endured one of Britain's cold-

Round houses, built by the villagers, proved surprisingly warm and roomy.

est winters in years without being troubled as most citizens were by power cuts. When 2 feet (0.6 meter) of snow fell, they just stayed in the round house with plenty of food and logs and got on with the weaving and wood carving.

The central fireplace was always the heart of the community. Here everyone sat round in the long winter evenings, talking or listening to one of the villagers play tunes on a six-stringed lyre—a kind of small harp.

Baths were taken in a big tub beside the fire. The water was warmed by plunging pieces of heated metal into it. If the water cooled, another piece of hot iron was dropped in. Hard scrubbing was necessary because the group's experiments at making soap out of animal fats were not successful.

Most things were done in leisurely fashion. The villagers quickly forgot the pace of modern life and lapsed into the slower rhythms of country people. No one had a watch, and although they built a sundial, they soon destroyed it because they found it tended to impose a schedule on them. "You'd look at it and think it's time for lunch," said Sharon

Village resident taking time from harvesting to inspect a scythe.

cellent bacon. The nine goats, stabled in their own miniature round house nearby, had been more obliging. They had produced 16 kids during the year, including two born that very morning. "We've really been very successful," said Kate, "because our sheep also had 13 lambs, and we've reared four calves." But the chickens strutting all over the place had been less agreeable. The BBC had thoughtfully provided a handsome Old English breed, but the Iron Agers found that these hens laid eggs only in the spring.

The meat available from their domestic animals was not enough. They added to it rabbits, squirrels, an occasional deer and sometimes even a rat, which was spit-roasted. The only trouble with rats, someone said, was that there was so little meat on them it was hardly worth the trouble.

Beyond the woods, the Iron Agers worked on 10 acres (4.05 hectares) of pasture and 5 acres (2.02 hectares) of cultivated land. They grew wheat, barley, oats, peas and tickbeans, all without benefit of modern pesticides or fertilizers. The harvest was so large that reaping it all became a real chore.

It took the villagers several

Preston, "but you might be busy and lunch might not be ready." Sunrise and sunset determined the shape of the day, especially in winter. "Life slowed down then," said John Rockcliff, who had once been a builder. "We almost hibernated, and felt tired without 12 hours' sleep."

But their achievements suggest they cannot have spent too much time lying around. While the beef stew grew tender in the cauldron, John and Kate Rossetti took me on a tour. Around the compound were thatched farm buildings. First we looked at the pigsty. Kate said the pigs had not reproduced, but they had made exdays to develop a good swing with their long-handled reaping hooks. And they found it frustrating to stop every two or three minutes to sharpen the soft iron blades. Yet in four weeks they cut, dried and carried 3½ tons of hay half a mile back to their village. They put it into six stacks, which provided some of the feed for their animals through the winter.

They concluded, however, that a true ancient settlement would have needed more land and larger flocks. As Jill Grainger told me, "We had 25 sheep, and that's not enough to clothe us. We estimate that at least 60 sheep would be necessary for a community of our size." Even so, they were all wearing clothing made from wool cut from their sheep with sharp flints. The wool was coarse and slightly greasy, but kept them warm and resisted the rain.

Indeed, their real worry was not clothes, but shoes. "The 20th-century thing we miss the most is footwear," said Jill, wriggling mud-caked bare feet before the round-house fire to thaw them out. "Going barefoot in winter mud is cripplingly cold. I think the Celts must have had shoes." At the beginning, the Iron Agers, following

Woman tending one of nine goats stabled in the village

the advice of archeologists, made shoes out of cowhide, pigskin and sheepskin. But these were not waterproof and wore out in a few days. Martin Elphick came up with the best solution. He made himself clogs from two strips of wood, each about one-half-inch thick, between which he fixed a strip of calf leather and then added leather uppers. They lasted well and elevated his feet out of at least some puddles.

Inventing footwear was only one example of the volunteers' experiments by trial and error to see how their Iron Age ancestors might have got along. "The most frustrating thing," said Peter Little, who proved to be one of the best craftsmen of the group, "was not being able to do things as well as the Celts. We could probably equal their skills in ten years, but in one year we're only just getting the hang of it."

Weeks were wasted, for instance, trying to make pottery because they not only had to build their own kiln, but had to learn exactly the right amount of ground-up stone or "grog" to put with the clay to make it bind correctly. The first pots crumbled to dust.

The Iron Agers proved more skillful at metalwork. They constructed a "forge" in which they swiftly found they could shape and weld iron. The real secret, John Rockcliff revealed, was a good pair of bellows, and he displayed what looked like a dirty old carpetbag. "We have been able to build up such heat," John said proudly, "that we can do almost anything on the forge."

The latter-day Iron Agers found that barter was essential to their whole survival. So they traded with the BBC team. Goat kids, a calf, pots, and baskets made from twigs were swapped for salt, eggs, cheese and honey. The volunteers had expected to be self-sufficient in

honey (they use a pound, or 0.5 kilogram, a day), but their modern bees did not take kindly to clay and straw hives and buzzed off to nearby trees. The honey harvest yielded only 40 pounds (18 kilograms), so there was no choice but to trade.

Meat formed a large part of their diet, which did not make eating easy for a few of the volunteers who were vegetarians. Indeed, the lack of much choice other than meat caused a lot of tension. Lindsay Ainsworth and her husband, for instance, loathed meat. On her days as cook she prepared only a vegetable menu. This led to friction between Lindsay and the rest of the group. The Ainsworths stayed on, but were forced to quit the village in December when their five-year-old son, Nicholas, became ill.

Although the Ainsworths' three children now look back on their Iron Age experiences as the "silly time," they adapted quickly to the freedom of the village life while they were there. Peter, the oldest, spent long hours wandering through the woods trying to trap animals. With his brother Nicholas, he even tried his hand at welding in the campfire. "Nicholas would take over the bellows at the forge and keep them going for hours," recalled Martin Elphick. "I am sure that in a real Iron Age village he would have been a blacksmith by the age of ten."

The satisfaction of learning to do things for themselves seems to have been a real reward, not just for the children but for everyone. "I've learned loads of practical things—looking after animals, weaving, even making my own home," said Jill Grainger.

The group had settled so well into the Iron Age that they had a sense of real regret at leaving their adopted village to travel 2300 years forward in time.

"We'd all have been ready to do it for another year if the money had been available," said Peter Little. The only thing they would have requested for a longer stay would have been some contact with family and friends. The BBC took them on a three-day outing to the sea during the summer, when they camped on the beach in a rough shelter. Otherwise their horizon was limited by the woods of their settlement.

The essence of the experiment would have been ruined if there had been weekends off

Without the luxury of toothbrushes, village residents learned a practical way to clean teeth.

Chicken taking a "dust bath" inside Iron Age kitchen door

at home to bathe, wear normal clothes and sleep in soft beds. Actually, Martin Elphick, a doctor before he went Iron Age, did sneak off for a two-day break on his own during the summer. He dug up some money he had buried in advance and hitchhiked to a sea-side town. There, still in Iron Age garb, he slept on the beach and treated himself to fish and chips. No one knew where he had gone, but after two days he was ready to return.

The villagers felt confined during the first few months as they adjusted to the slow, pastoral life of the Iron Age community. But after 12 months in the wild, they seemed to feel their new way of life had become their normal one.

What can really be learned from the Iron Age project has been debated by archeologists. But at least one long-standing mystery was solved for one archeologist when he noticed just inside the door of the round house a shallow depression of scooped-out earth. He remembered that he had found this same depression at every Iron Age site he had ever dug. Archeologists had always questioned whether there was some religious meaning to this strange hollow in the ground. He asked the villagers how their depression came into being. Oh, they replied, whenever the chickens strutted in out of the rain, they took a dust bath just inside the door. They had worn away quite an interesting-looking hollow, hadn't they?

Number of Words: 2750 ÷ _____ Minutes Reading Time = Rate _____

I. MAIN IDEA

Check √ the statement that best describes what the selection is about.

_____ **1.** A group of Britons found life in an Iron Age village not very different from life in the 20th century.

_____ **2.** A group of people has found it very difficult to go back to nature and live like Iron Age Celts.

_____ **3.** A group of 20-century people managed to live somewhat like Iron Age Celts.

10 points for correct answer   SCORE: _____

II. SKIMMING

Skim the selection to find the information needed to complete each statement below. Circle the letter of each correct answer.

1. The group taking part in the Iron Age experiment was made up of _____ .
   a. 25 people   **b.** 15 people   **c.** 100 people

2. The group started the experiment in _____ .
   a. December 1977   **b.** March 1977   **c.** July 1977

3. The group tried to imitate Celtic village life of _____ .
   a. 2300 years ago   **b.** 300 years ago
                              c. the 25th century

4. The main round house they lived in was _____ .
   a. 16 feet across and 13 feet high
   b. 48 feet across and 30 feet high
   c. 75 feet across and 50 feet high

5. To have enough wool for clothes, the group would have needed _____ .
   a. 25 sheep   **b.** 60 sheep   **c.** 100 sheep

8 points for each correct answer   SCORE: _____

III. CRITICAL THINKING

Decide whether each statement below is based on fact or reflects the author's opinion. Write F for fact and O for opinion.

_____ **1.** Iron Age people are more skillful than modern men.

_____ **2.** Life during the Iron Age was harder than it is today.

_____ **3.** People are able to adapt to a new way of life.

_____ **4.** It is better to be alive now than during the Iron Age.

10 points for each correct answer   SCORE: _____

IV. INFERENCES

Check √ the statement that can most accurately be inferred from the selection.

_____ **1.** The BBC developed the project as an amusement.

_____ **2.** The volunteers were all strange people.

_____ **3.** The project succeeded in approximating the conditions in which Iron Age people lived.

_____ **4.** The project failed to show anything significant.

10 points for correct answer   SCORE: _____

PERFECT TOTAL SCORE: 100   TOTAL SCORE: _____

V. QUESTIONS FOR THOUGHT

What are some of the major problems you would have had participating in the Iron Age experiment? What would have helped you solve these problems?

Campy's Unforgettable Courage

Howard A. Rusk, M.D.

Roy Campanella tagging out opposing team member at home plate

During the 1950s, before the Dodgers moved from Brooklyn to Los Angeles, I became a real baseball fan. And, to me, the player who stood out among all the rest was Roy Campanella. Campy, as we fans fondly called him, was a clever and scrappy catcher. With a runner leaving first base to steal second, Campy would spring from behind the plate like a young tiger and fire the ball to second like a bullet. Often the runner hadn't a chance.

And, in those days, this half-black, half-Italian, from the sandlots in Philadelphia, was probably the best-hitting catcher in baseball. In 1953, one of his best years, Campy set three major-league records for catchers: the most home runs (41), runs batted in (142) and putouts (807). These achievements, plus a batting average of .312, earned him the National League's Most Valuable Player award that year. "When I can no longer wear the uniform," he told reporters later, "they might as well bury me, 'cause I'll be dead."

But when I first met Campy, less than five years later, he wasn't wearing the uniform, and I knew he never would again. His car had skidded on ice and crashed into a telephone pole. Campy was thrown under the dashboard and broke his neck. Emergency surgery probably saved his life, but his spinal cord had been severed. He was paralyzed from the shoulders down. As director of New York University's Institute of Rehabilitation Medicine, which specializes in working with the spine-injured and the paralyzed, I was asked to see him.

I'll never forget how Campy looked lying there in the hospital bed. His tough muscles were still hard, but his body was as unresponsive as stone. He had slight movement in his wrists and could extend and bend his arms but not his fingers. And those anxious eyes were filled with questions about the future.

Sitting on the edge of his bed after examining him, I spoke gently. "Campy, I don't know whether you're going to get a little back, a lot back—or nothing. Only time will tell. We'll start to train you tomorrow, but there's no magic in this. You will have to work harder than you ever have in your whole life."

"I'm ready," he said.

Next day we moved him into Room 414 at the Institute, his home for the next six months. With agonizing effort he learned to sit up, first in bed, then in a wheelchair. Then, clumsily, he learned to feed

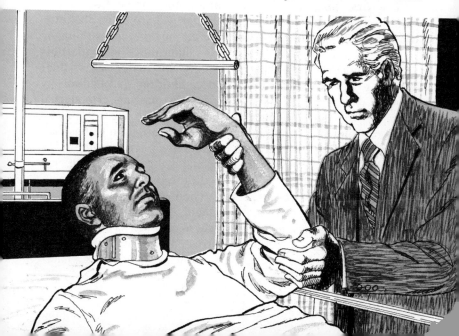

himself with a fork or spoon held in a slotted leather wristband. Day after day he was strapped to a tilt board to promote circulation in his feet. He suffered through torturous periods on the treatment table learning to roll over and spent exhausting sessions at the weight machines to strengthen his feeble wrists.

Sometimes I wondered if Campy would ever make it. He was a man who loved speed and action and bone-jarring slides to the plate. He needed to catch and throw, jaw it out with the umpire and smash a ball over the fence to the roar of the crowd. Did he have inner strength enough to rebuild his life anew?

The first hint that he did came one evening as I heard Campy talking on the telephone. "Hello," he was saying. "Is this the Dodger clubhouse? I want to speak to John Roseboro." Then, "John? This is Campy. I've been watching you play on television and, John, you're crowding the plate too much." Campy listened for a moment while John talked. Then he said, "Everybody gets in a slump sometime, but that's no time to feel sorry for yourself. You can't just quit; you got to try all the harder."

I walked on then, knowing that Campy was coming back. He'd dug down and, somewhere, found a new kind of courage.

Patiently, he continued his painful exercises, never complaining. Toward the end of the year, the star athlete who could no longer walk had begun to inspire hope and courage in the other patients. He'd talk baseball with them, or he'd get them talking about themselves, or he'd tell them about his own accident and how he thought his world had come to an end. But it was all different now. Campy believed in his own future, and he made others believe in theirs.

Late that fall, in a wheelchair and a neck brace, Campy was discharged from the Institute. For all the odds against him, he was determined to support his family—his wife Ruthe, their three children and her son by a former marriage. He started his own radio show, *Campy's Corner,* a program of baseball interviews, and accepted a spring-training coaching job with the Dodgers.

Then came another blow. David, his 15-year-old stepson, whom he loved as his own, was arrested on a burglary charge. Campy was heartsick. There

Campanella posing from wheelchair with wife Roxie and Baseball Commissioner Bowie Kuhn, September 1978

was a second offense, and a third; it was deeply upsetting. He spent long hours with the boy trying to give him the father's love and support that David needed. It was a bad time for both, but it worked.

Campy told me about it later. He'd come into the office for a checkup, and I said I'd seen the stories in the papers. For a moment he looked down at his helpless body, imprisoned in a wheelchair. Then he raised his head, smiled a quiet smile, and said the most moving thing I ever heard a patient say.

"You know, doctor, this trouble my boy was in." He spoke slowly, reaching for the right words. "I know that breaking your neck is a tough way to learn a lesson, but lying in bed, paralyzed, I learned two things: tolerance and patience, toward myself and everybody else." He hesitated. "That's love—isn't it?"

Not long after, Campy's wife, from whom he had recently separated, died. It was a tragic time for Campy. Some years later, he married his present wife, Roxie, and together they kept the family going.

Never once did he let anyone feel sorry for him. He told me how he and Roxie would go out to dinner, dances and other social events. "It makes me feel great," he said. "I know everybody has problems, but people look at me and get the feeling that if a guy in a wheelchair can have such a good time, they can't be so bad off, after all."

In the summer of 1976, Campy called me and said he was in deep trouble. His bedsores, a constant problem caused by impaired circulation, were worse than ever. Moreover, he had developed other complications. We hospitalized him at once. Before we were through, he had to have seven surgical procedures, with skin grafts and dozens of blood transfusions. He stayed with us for more than a year. Most of the time he had to lie flat on his face, in a special frame in which he could be turned over

several times a day. Again, he never complained.

One night as I was leaving his room, something made me turn back. "Campy," I said, "here you are, back where you were almost 20 years ago. Yet you still manage to be cheerful, uncomplaining, helpful to others and full of plans. Tell me, what keeps you going?"

"Well," he said, "I go back to the Scripture my momma taught us when we were kids in Philadelphia, the Twenty-third Psalm: 'The Lord is my shepherd; I shall not want.' I say it over and over."

The first time, he said, was right after the accident. With his broken neck, he was already in bad shape. Then he contracted pneumonia. "I was in an oxygen tent, but I couldn't breathe right. The doctor said, 'Campy, the only thing I can do is cut a hole in your throat and insert a tube. It'll help you breathe. But I can't give you any anesthetic.'

"I was feeling so bad, I just thought of Momma, and how she taught us to get down on our knees and say that psalm; and while he operated on me, I kept sayin' it over and over in my head. The next day I was all right. The tube was in. There was no pain.

"Roxie and I have taught that passage to our kids, and they have taught it to theirs. I say it every night in bed before I go to sleep. And when I'm out of bed and don't feel right, I say it again. So many times it has pulled me through."

When we released him from our care, Campy didn't waste much time getting on the phone. More than anything now, he wanted to go back to work. There might be something he could do in public relations, he thought, with the New York Mets. (As it turned out, there was.)

Some months ago, my office door opened and there was Campy in his wheelchair—cheerful, feeling good again, looking ahead. He'd come in for a checkup. He told me that he and Roxie intended to move to California. They like warm weather—and they'd be closer to his beloved Dodgers, the one team of his major league career.

"I'm having a wonderful second life," Campy told me. "I want to tell everybody about it. I want them to remember that when trouble comes, it ain't always bad. Take it with a smile, do the best you can and the good Lord will help you out."

To me, this is Campy—Campy of the fighting heart, the Roy Campanella I'll always remember. His neck was broken, but never his spirit.

Campanella, assisted by two young friends, officially starts National Awareness Week (June 30 through July 6) for handicapped

Campanella throws out first ball of 1978 World Series between Dodgers and Yankees with able support from Don Newcombe, former Dodger pitcher.

Number of Words: 1615 ÷ _____ Minutes Reading Time = Rate _____

I. INFERENCES

Campy says: "Breaking your neck is a tough way to learn a lesson, but lying in bed I learned tolerance and patience." Check √ the two conclusions below that can be inferred from this statement.

_____ **1.** Campy has reached the point where he can accept his accident and its consequences.

_____ **2.** Campy has learned that he is not responsible for anything that happens to him.

_____ **3.** By learning more about himself, Campy has become more understanding of other people.

_____ **4.** His accident has given Campy many money-making opportunities.

10 points for each correct answer   SCORE: _____

II. AUTHOR'S PURPOSE

Check √ four statements below that reveal how the author makes the reader admire Campy's character and vitality.

_____ **1.** He shows us Campy's deep love of life.

_____ **2.** He compares Campy's life to that of other athletes.

_____ **3.** He describes Campy's spiritual strength.

_____ **4.** He gives us examples of Campy's courage.

_____ **5.** He tells us of Campy's struggle against depression.

_____ **6.** He shows Campy's determination to rehabilitate himself.

10 points for each correct answer   SCORE: _____

III. GENERALIZATIONS

The selection tells a great many things about the life of a handicapped person. Check √ four statements below that are generally true of such a life.

_____ **1.** Handicapped people prefer to live in hospitals.

_____ **2.** Overcoming a handicap can present enormous difficulties and require agonizing physical efforts.

_____ **3.** The struggle to overcome a handicap can also be an opportunity to find new strength within oneself.

_____ **4.** A handicapped person can become an inspiration to others.

_____ **5.** A handicapped person can lead a full life: have a job, a family, plans for the future. . . .

_____ **6.** The feelings of a handicapped person are different from those of "normal" people.

_____ **7.** Most handicapped persons lead richer lives than people without handicaps.

10 points for each correct answer   SCORE: _____

PERFECT TOTAL SCORE: 100   TOTAL SCORE: _____

IV. QUESTIONS FOR THOUGHT

How has this story helped you understand handicapped people better? How has it helped you?

Crowds enjoying the conveniences of Montreal's underground city . . .

UNDERGROUND CITY OF THE FUTURE

J.D. Ratcliff

Are cities doomed to be noisy, dangerous places of filth, fumes and strangling traffic? Not this one! Here it never rains; the temperature never varies from a comfortable 72° Fahrenheit (22° Celsius). There is pure air to breathe, and there are no screeching motor sounds. It's a city of the future: underground Montreal in Canada.

... while, on the ground above, city residents brave the snow and cold.

There may be 30 inches (76 centimeters) of snow on the ground (Montreal averages 108 inches, or 274 centimeters a year), but under the icy streets you may stroll, coatless, through several miles of attractive promenade. Choose among more than 300 varied and attractive shops, a dozen cinemas and theaters, 62 restaurants, snack bars and sidewalk cafes. There is no feeling of being confined in a tunnel. You wander on broad, traffic-free avenues up to 36 feet (11 meters) wide. Lighting is bright and imaginative. One plaza has leafless trees softly lighted. Another has a colorful glass sculpture—the largest in the world.

In this dazzling underground city, you can buy groceries, have a sauna bath, buy a suit of armor or a canary. You want to be married? Several shops sell wedding dresses, and you can enter a church without setting foot in the snow. You could work and play here a lifetime—in connecting hotel, apartment and office buildings—and only have to surface to be buried (there is no mortuary).

As long as cities have existed, they have been associated with din, dirt, confusion. Almost 500 years ago, Leonardo da Vinci had a new idea for big-city traffic problems. He suggested having carts at street level, pedestrians on elevated walkways. Modern city planners agree that traffic should be separated. Trains and subways could be at one under-street level, parking at another and walkways at a third. But costs and mechanical difficulties stood in the way. You could not, the experts said, build a new city *under* one already in existence. Then a unique situation arose in Montreal.

The core area of the city was a sad sight. Old buildings surrounded a 7-acre (3-hectare) eyesore, known as "the hole." This "hole" was the pit-yards of Canadian National Rail-

ways. For years railroad officials had talked of developing this dismal area. Finally, in 1956, they began by calling in city planners.

The first proposal was for a group of buildings with a cross-shaped skyscraper to be built over the pit. But one of the planners, Vincent Ponte, had a better idea. He saw here a chance to build the weather-proof underground city he had long dreamed of.

Ponte explained that as new buildings rose, they could tie into the underground city. Thus it would eventually

A drawing by Leonardo da Vinci of a plan (never executed) for a model city.

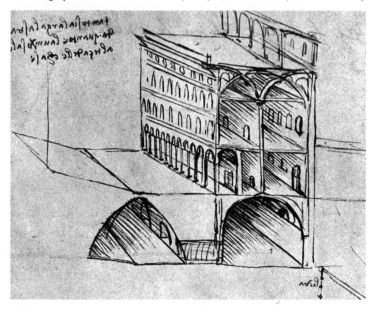

Place Ville Marie continues to attract satisfied customers to its comfortable underground promenade.

spread, rootlike, under most of the city's 200-acre (80-hectare) core. It would link four large hotels, two railroad stations, three giant department stores and underground garages with space for 10,000 cars. It was an exciting dream.

Naturally, there were objections. Critics, thinking of tiled tunnels, asked: wouldn't people shun under-street shops? They hadn't in the 17-acre (7-hectare) area under New York's Rockefeller Center, Ponte replied. After all, people didn't like being splashed with salt slush in winter or seared in summer. Wouldn't people feel hemmed in, confined? Not, said Ponte, if "streets" were wide enough and attractively lighted.

When Place Ville Marie, as it was called, opened in 1962, the popularity of underground living in weatherproof comfort was instant. Other giant complexes began to rise in the area. Ponte helped to plan the huge substructure that would connect each with his growing underground city. Place Bonaventure, one of the largest commercial buildings in the world, opened in 1967. Since it sits

Passengers prepare to board Montreal's metro, one of world's cleanest and quietest subway systems.

on a slope, the depth of the underground part varies. In one place it goes down eight stories. Ponte provided two shopping levels—totaling 5½ acres (2 hectares)—ramps and docks capable of handling anything up to 60-foot (18 meters) truck-trailer rigs, garage space for 1000 cars.

As new sections hooked into the underground city, the idea caught on in surrounding areas. A mile (1.6 kilometers) from the city core, a magnificent square shot up. It had two apartment towers, one office building and, of course, a be-low-street area for shops, restaurants and a cinema. This, in turn, connected with nearby Alexis Nihon Plaza. Here there were three shopping levels, two parking levels and even a public "square."

At the beginning it was feared that this vast growth in Montreal's center would bring on a transportation crisis—drawing tens of thousands of office workers and visitors into a limited area. In a curious way it *prevented* it. For years Montreal had wanted a subway but lacked funds to build one. New taxes provided by the sky-

111

scrapers enabled the city to build one of the world's finest metros, with quiet, spotless, rubber-tired cars.

So the spreading underground city helped get people and cars off the streets. It is also adding new dimensions to living—not the least of which is safety. Criminals apparently don't like brightly lighted places where there is no place to hide and no safe place to hide parked cars to transport stolen goods.

Ponte sees the underground concept as the savior of cities all over the world. Controlled environment is as attractive in the tropics as in the wintry north. But things probably won't move as fast elsewhere as they have in Montreal, for the simple reason that ownership of a huge tract of land by a single organization is rare. Buying property one piece at a time can be costly and time-consuming. Also, the cost of digging under existing buildings, plus engineering problems involved,

Underground visitors enjoying metro transportation that adds new dimensions to their lives.

Passengers are content to wait for train in the attractive station.

may rule out this approach.

Is the door then closed for others? By no means. Space under parks may be used. And Ponte has a dazzling idea for New York City. There are two levels of railroad tracks under Park Avenue (a wide street that runs down the middle of Manhattan Island), but with today's reduced rail traffic one is enough. Why not use the upper level for an all-weather shopping promenade? The idea is both interesting and attractive.

Ponte has worked on plans for other cities in the United States, as well as other countries. It appears that from now on almost any city can come in out of the cold—or heat. Man, who emerged from the cave a few thousand years ago, may now be returning to it—but with a quiet, attractive, pleasurable difference.

Number of Words: 1085 ÷ _____ Minutes Reading Time = Rate _____

I. FACT/OPINION

Write F for each sentence that states a fact. Write O for each sentence that states an opinion.

_____ **1.** Cities are always dangerous places of filth, fumes and strangling traffic.

_____ **2.** The temperature in an underground city can be kept at a level that is always pleasant.

_____ **3.** Underground Montreal offers almost anything a person might want to buy or do.

_____ **4.** People in an underground city feel hemmed in, confined.

_____ **5.** It is difficult and time-consuming to build an undergound city.

_____ **6.** The underground concept is the savior of cities everywhere.

5 points for each correct answer   SCORE: _____

II. CAUSE/EFFECT

Underground Montreal has proved very successful. Match each cause of this success (column A) with its effect (column B).

A	B
_____ **1.** A subway system has been built.	**a.** It is very popular.
_____ **2.** Many new buildings are linked to it.	**b.** Thieves stay away from it.
_____ **3.** It offers weatherproof comfort.	**c.** Traffic jams have been prevented.
_____ **4.** The city is brightly lighted.	**d.** It keeps growing.

10 points for each correct answer   SCORE: _____

III. GENERALIZATIONS

The selection presents a positive view of underground cities. If you wished to show an unfavorable picture, which statements below would you be likely to make? Check √ three.

_____ **1.** Living and working underground can make people feel cut off from the "real" world.

_____ **2.** People cannot live without the excitement of shops, restaurants, theaters and crowds.

_____ **3.** Being exposed to nature (sunlight, trees, fields, rivers . . .) is an important part of life.

_____ **4.** A way of life that depends on underground cities requires huge amounts of energy.

_____ **5.** Underground cities can be built to control pollution.

_____ **6.** Science has proven that people are not dependent upon nature.

_____ **7.** Where a person wants to live is a matter of personal taste.

10 points for each correct answer   SCORE: _____

PERFECT TOTAL SCORE: 100   TOTAL SCORE: _____

IV. QUESTIONS FOR THOUGHT

Would you want an underground city built where you live? What would be its advantages? Its disadvantages?

Shaving

Leslie Norris

Earlier, when Barry had left the house to go to the game, a frost had still been thick on the roads. But the brisk April sun had soon dispersed it, and now he could feel the spring warmth on his back through the thick tweed of his coat. His left arm was beginning to stiffen up where he'd jarred it in a tackle, but it was nothing serious. He moved his shoulders against the tightness of his jacket and was surprised again by the unexpected weight of his muscles, the thickening strength of his body. A few years back, he thought, he had been a small, unimportant boy, one of a group, hardly aware that he was a person in his own right. But time had changed him. He was tall, strongly made; his hands and feet were adult and heavy. The rooms in which all his life he'd moved had grown too small for him. Sometimes a devouring restlessness drove him from the house to walk

long distances in the dark. He hardly understood how it had happened. Amused and quiet, he walked the High Street among the morning shoppers.

He saw Jackie Bevan across the road and remembered how, when they were both six years old, Jackie had swallowed a pin. The flustered teachers had clucked about Jackie as he stood there, crying, cheeks awash with tears, his nose wet. But now Jackie was tall and cool, his thick, pale hair sleekly combed, his gray suit sharp. He was talking to a girl as golden as a daffodil.

"Hey, hey!" called Jackie. "How's the athlete, how's Barry boy?"

He waved a graceful hand at Barry.

"Come and talk to Sue," he said.

Barry shifted his bag to his left hand and walked over, forming in his mind the answers he'd make to Jackie's questions.

117

"Did we win?" Jackie asked. "Was the old Barry Stanford magic at work this morning? What was the score? Give us an account, Barry, without modesty or delay. This is Sue, by the way."

"I've seen you about," the girl said.

"You could hardly miss him," said Jackie. "Four men, roped together, spent a week climbing him—they thought he was Mt. Everest. He ought to carry a warning beacon, he's a danger to aircraft."

"Silly," said the girl, smiling at Jackie. "He's not much taller than you are."

She had a nice voice too.

"We won," Barry said. "Seventeen points to three, and it was a good game. The ground was hard, though."

He could think of nothing else to say.

"Let's all go for a cup of coffee," Jackie said. "Let's celebrate your safe return."

"I don't think so," Barry said. "Thanks. I'll go straight home."

"Okay," said Jackie, rocking on his heels so that the sun could shine on his smile. "How's your father?"

"No better," Barry said, "He's not going to get better."

"Yes, well," said Jackie, serious and uncomfortable, "tell him my mother and father ask about him."

"I will," Barry promised. "He'll be pleased."

Barry dropped the bag in the front hall and moved into the room that had been the dining room until his father's illness. His father lay in the white bed, his long body thin, his still head scarcely denting the pillow. He seemed asleep, thin blue lids covering his eyes. But when Barry turned away, he spoke.

"Hullo, son," he said. "Did you win?"

His voice was a dry, light rustling, hardly louder than the breath that carried it. Its sound moved Barry almost to tears, but he stepped close to the bed and looked down at the dying man.

"Yes," he said. "We won fairly easily. It was a good game."

His father lay with his eyes closed, his breath irregular and shallow.

"Did you score?" he asked.

"Twice," Barry said. "I had a try in each half."

He thought of the easy way in which he'd caught the ball before his second try; casually, he had taken it on the tips of his fingers, on his full charge for the line, breaking the fullback's tackle. Nobody could have stopped him. But watching his father's weakness he felt humble and ashamed, as if the morning's game was not worth talking about. His father's face, fine-skinned and pale, carried a dark stubble of beard, almost a week's growth, and his hair stuck out over his brow.

"Good," said his father, after a long pause. "I'm glad it was a good game."

Barry's mother bustled about the kitchen.

"Your father's not well," she said. "He's down today, feels depressed. He's a particular man, your father. He feels dirty with all that beard on him."

She slammed shut the stove door.

"Mr. Cleaver was supposed to come up and shave him," she said, "and that was three days ago. Little things have always worried your father. Every detail must be perfect for him."

Barry filled a glass with milk from the refrigerator. He was very thirsty.

"I'll shave him," he said.

His mother stopped, her head on one side.

"Do you think you can?" she asked. "He'd like it if you can."

"I can do it," Barry said.

He washed his hands as carefully as a surgeon. His father's razor was in a blue leather case. Barry unfastened the clasp and took out the razor. It had not been properly cleaned after its last use, and lather had stiffened on it. There were rust stains, brown as chocolate, on the surface of the blade. Barry removed it, throwing it in the wastebin. He washed the razor until it glistened, and dried it on a soft towel. He took a new blade from its envelope, the paper clinging to the thin metal. The blade was smooth to the touch. Barry slipped it into the grip of the razor, making it tight in the head.

The shaving soap, hard and white, was kept in a wooden bowl. Barry could almost see his father in the days of his health, standing before his mirror, thick white lather on his face and neck. As a little boy, Barry had loved the perfume of the soap, had waited for his father to lift the razor to his face, for one careful stroke to take away the white suds.

His father's shaving mug was a thick cup, plain and serviceable. A gold line ran outside the rim of the cup; another inside, just below the lip. Its handle was large and sturdy, and the face of the mug carried a portrait of the young Queen Elizabeth II. And beneath that in small black letters, ran the words: "Coronation June 2nd 1953." The cup was much older than Barry. A pattern of faint cracks, fine as a web, had worked itself through the white glaze. Inside, on the bottom, a few dark bristles were lying, loose and dry. Barry shook them out, then held the cup in his hand, feeling its solidness. Then he washed it ferociously until it was beautifully clean.

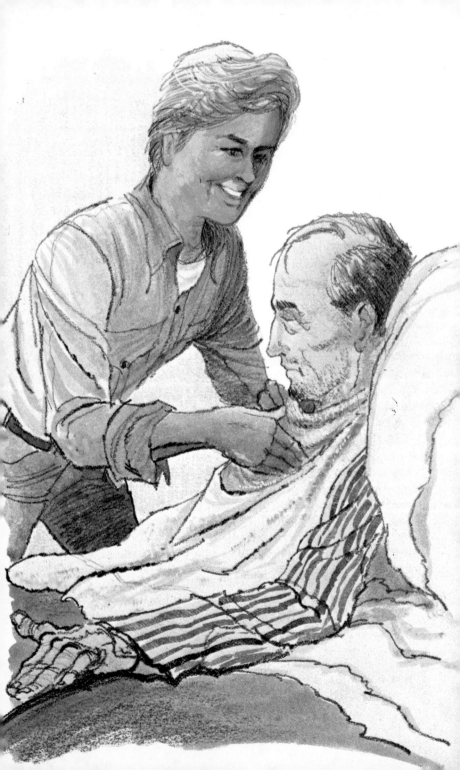

He set everything on a tray—razor, soap, brush, towels. Testing the hot water with a finger, he filled the mug and put that, too, on the tray. Then he went downstairs, carrying the tray with one hand.

His father was waiting for him. Barry set the tray on a bedside table and bent over his father, sliding an arm under the man's thin shoulders, lifting him so that he sat against the high pillows.

"By heaven, you're strong," his father said softly. He was as breathless as if he'd been running.

"So are you," said Barry.

"I was," his father said. "I used to be strong once."

He sat exhausted against the pillows.

"We'll wait a bit," Barry said.

"You could have used your electric razor," his father said. "I expected that."

"You wouldn't like it," Barry said. "You'll get a closer shave this way."

He placed the large towel about his father's shoulders.

"Now," he said, smiling down.

The water was hot in the cup. Barry wet the brush and worked up the lather. Gently he built up a covering of soft foam on the man's chin and his stark cheekbones.

"You're using a lot of soap," his father said.

"Not too much," Barry said. "You've got a lot of beard."

His father lay there quietly, his wasted arms at his sides.

"It's comforting," he said. "You'd be surprised how comforting it is."

Barry took up the razor, weighing it in his hand, thinking about how he'd use it. He felt confident.

"If you have any prayers to say," he said.

"I've said a lot of prayers," his father answered.

Barry leaned over and placed the razor against his father's face. He held the razor in the tips of his fingers and drew the blade sweetly through the lather. The new edge moved light as a touch over the hardness of the upper jaw and down to the chin, sliding away the beard easily. He sighed as he shook the razor in the hot water, washing away the soap.

"How's it going?" his father asked.

"No problem," Barry said. "You needn't worry."

It was as if he had never known what his father really looked like. He was discovering, under his hands, the clear bones of the face and head. They became sharp and recognizable under his fingers. When he moved his father's face a gentle inch to one side, he touched with his fingers the frail temples, the blue veins of his father's life. With the ut-

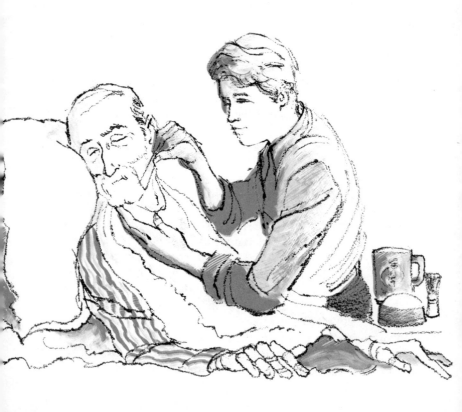

most care he took away the hair from his father's face.

"Now for your neck," he said. "We might as well do the job properly."

"You've got good hands," his father said. "You can trust those hands, they won't ever let you down."

Barry held his father's head in his left arm, so that the man could lean back his head, exposing the throat. He brushed fresh lather under the chin. His father's throat was fleshless and vulnerable; his head was a hard weight on the boy's arm. Barry was filled with a protective love. He lifted the razor and began to shave.

"You don't have to worry," he said. "Not at all. Not about anything."

He held his father in the bend of his strong arm, and they looked at each other. Their heads were very close.

"How old are you?" his father said.

"Seventeen," Barry said. "Near enough seventeen."

"You're young," his father said, "to have this happen."

"Not too young," Barry said. "I'm bigger than most men."

"I think you are," his father said.

He leaned his head tiredly against the boy's shoulder. He was without strength; his face was cold and smooth. He had let go all his authority, handed it over. He lay back on his pillow, knowing his weakness, and looked at his son with wonder, with a curious pride.

"I won't worry then," he said. "About anything."

"There's no need," Barry said. "Why should you have to."

He wiped his father's face clean of all soap with a damp towel. The smell of illness was everywhere, overpowering even the perfumed shaving soap. Barry settled his father down and took away the shaving tools, putting them away with the same care with which he'd prepared them: the cleaned and glittering razor in its broken case; the soap, its bowl wiped and dried, on the shelf between the brush and the mug. He washed his hands and scrubbed his nails. His hands were firm and broad, pink after their scrubbing. The fingers were short and strong, the little fingers slightly crooked. Soft dark hair grew on the backs of his hands and his fingers just above the knuckles. Not long ago they had been small bare hands; not very long ago.

Barry opened wide the bathroom window. Already, although it was not yet two o'clock, the sun was moving and people were walking quickly, wrapped in their heavy coats against the cold that was to come. But now the window was full in the beam of the dying sunlight, and Barry stood there, lit by its golden warmth for a whole minute, knowing it would soon be gone.

Number of Words: 2031 ÷ _____ Minutes Reading Time = Rate _____

I. STORY ELEMENTS

Put a check √ before the best ending for each sentence.

1. This story could best be described as
   _____ **a.** a look at the way tragedy can affect a family.
   _____ **b.** a good description of how to shave an older person.
   _____ **c.** an in-depth study of a dread disease.
2. The mood of the story is
   _____ **a.** noisy and happy.
   _____ **b.** sad and quiet.
   _____ **c.** suspenseful.
3. In this story we are made to appreciate
   _____ **a.** the beauty of the earth around us.
   _____ **b.** the excitement of living life to the fullest.
   _____ **c.** the courage of a maturing young man.

10 points for each correct answer   SCORE:_____

II. INFERENCES

Put a check √ before the best ending for each sentence.

1. Barry did not go for coffee with Jackie and Sue because he
   _____ **a.** didn't like being with either one of them.
   _____ **b.** wasn't in the mood for wisecracks and gaiety.
   _____ **c.** had to go home and shave his father.
2. Barry felt that the game was not worth discussing because
   _____ **a.** it seemed unimportant next to his father's illness.
   _____ **b.** his father was too weak to care.
   _____ **c.** they had won too easily.
3. Barry cleaned the shaving tools because he
   _____ **a.** was afraid of getting germs on his father.
   _____ **b.** hated to touch anything dirty.
   _____ **c.** was performing an act of love for his father.

10 points for each correct answer   SCORE:_____

III. CRITICAL THINKING

Circle the letter of the statement in each group below that most fully expresses the author's feelings.

1. **a.** He washed the cup ferociously until it was beautifully clean.
   b. He held the cup in his hand.
   c. He filled the mug and put it, too, on the tray.
2. **a.** "I've seen you about," the girl said.
   b. "Come and talk to Sue," Jackie said.
   c. He was talking to a girl as golden as a daffodil.
3. **a.** Not long ago they had been small bare hands; not very long ago.
   b. He washed his hands and scrubbed his nails.
   c. His hands were pink after their scrubbing.
4. **a.** Barry held his father's head in his left arm.
   b. His father's head was a hard weight on the boy's arm.
   c. Barry was filled with a protective love.
5. **a.** Barry filled a glass with milk from the refrigerator.
   b. He sighed as he shook the razor in the hot water, washing away the soap.
   c. Barry took up the razor, weighing it in his hand, thinking about how he'd use it.

8 points for each correct answer   SCORE:_____

PERFECT TOTAL SCORE: 100   TOTAL SCORE_____

IV. QUESTIONS FOR THOUGHT

What techniques did the author use to create the mood of the story? Were they effective? Why?